JOHN SAINTY

LAST MAN STANDING

JOHN SAINTY

LAST MAN STANDING

from Saint to Saints and Beyond

WITH

NEIL VACHER

pitch

First published by Pitch Publishing, 2025

Pitch Publishing
9 Donnington Park,
85 Birdham Road,
Chichester, West Sussex,
PO20 7AJ
www.pitchpublishing.co.uk
info@pitchpublishing.co.uk

A CIP catalogue record is available for this book from the British Library.

ISBN 978 1 80150 927 5

MIX
Paper | Supporting responsible forestry
FSC™ C016779

Printed and bound on FSC® certified paper in line with our continuing commitment to ethical business practices, sustainability and the environment.

Typesetting and origination by Pitch Publishing

Printed and bound in India by Replika Press Pvt. Ltd.

CONTENTS

DEDICATION

To my grandad, Johann Albert Bolten, Merchant Navy, British Empire Medal for Meritorious Service, to all those below, and to every football player, coach, manager and scout.

It may not be true,
I wouldn't know what to do,
If I was the last man standing
Too many friends have gone and died,
I would be telling a lie,
If I said I wanted to be,
The last man standing.

Jimmy (Neighbour), Roger (Smith), Keith (Weller) all friends younger than me,
Have long gone and I cannot see why,
Terrible things should have happened to them,
The ultimate sacrifice – to die.

John AKA **'The Saint'**

Last Man Standing: John Sainty, from Saint to Saints and Beyond is the story of a man who dedicated his life to football. A former player, coach, manager, director and scout, John Sainty often operated 'beneath the radar' but was well respected by the game's senior figures. He held simple philosophies on football and life. Schooled as a player in the 1960s at Tottenham, his coaching ability was spotted at Bournemouth by John Bond, whom he followed to Norwich and Manchester City, where his measured approach proved an ideal foil to the brashness of Bond. In the 1990s, he assisted Danny Bergara and Dave Jones at Stockport before Jones took him to Southampton, where he later became academy director, with the likes of Gareth Bale, Adam Lallana and James Ward-Prowse all passing through his care in their formative years. Sadly, in recent years, John suffered from the early stages of dementia and suddenly passed away before this book was completed, but with the help of his former colleagues, this labour of love has now been fulfilled.

FOREWORD by DENNIS TUEART

I FIRST came across John Sainty when I was a player at Manchester City, and he arrived as first-team coach under manager John Bond in 1980. At that time, City were having a disastrous run and the situation was quite desperate for us, but we eventually turned things around, comfortably avoiding relegation from the First Division and reaching the Centenary FA Cup Final the following year, albeit eventually losing to Spurs in a replay.

Our success that season came through playing organised, open, attacking and entertaining football, which was paramount in John's coaching philosophy. I was fascinated to see where John Sainty's career would take him after leaving City and it did not surprise me at all that he was appointed to several managerial positions before becoming assistant manager to Danny Bergara and Dave Jones at Stockport County. He then became part of a particularly successful period in the club's history.

I could fully understand why Dave Jones was delighted to then take John with him to Southampton, initially as his assistant and then to set up that club's academy as its first academy director. John accumulated a vast knowledge during his time in the professional game and possessed all-round abilities which enabled him to successfully cover a wide range of positions, and his ability to communicate well with younger players, in particular, would have made him ideal for this particular role.

I was delighted to be involved in a small part of John's career and he was a great help to me, both as a coach and in my recovery from a serious Achilles tendon injury, constantly encouraging me throughout my rehabilitation programme. Although he was not one to court the limelight, John's ability was well-recognised within the game of football and by all those who were lucky enough to come into contact with him. I am delighted that this book has been produced to provide us with a lasting memory of him.

Dennis Tueart

Dennis Tueart was a member of Sunderland's FA Cup-winning side of 1973 and scored 46 goals in 178 league appearances for the Wearsiders before moving to Manchester City in 1974. After featuring in City's League Cup triumph in 1976, he briefly moved to the United States and helped New York Cosmos win the Soccer Bowl in 1978 before returning to City two years later. Dennis spent a further four years at Maine Road and was a substitute in the replay of the 1981 FA Cup Final. Dennis made 224 league appearances during his two spells with City, scoring 86 goals and also gained six full international caps for England. He later became a director of the club, his departure in 2007 ending a 33-year association as a player and director.

INTRODUCTION
by LINDSAY SAINTY

IT FEELS completely alien to be known as a widow, as I still expect John to come walking through the door, then the jolt to reality takes hold.

How fortunate I now feel to complete this book along with Neil, who first came to our aid before John's 70th birthday when I rang AFC Bournemouth in the hope of obtaining some photos of John to add to a picture board for celebrations at his party. Neil invited me along to the club and some brilliant photos were found. During our conversation, I mentioned John's book and Neil offered his help. This led to some pleasant meetings for the three of us at Neil's invitation to the Vitality Stadium, with the result of almost finalising the chapters when John so suddenly and unexpectedly died.

Through working together with John over the years on this project I have learned even more about John's time at his various clubs. And from all the wonderful tributes included in each chapter, the words that come across most vividly are 'calm' and 'help', which sum up John's character perfectly. He never raised his voice, was always quiet and unassuming, but had that mischievous twinkle in his eye, a quick wit, sharp mind, generous heart and a naughty sense of humour.

He rarely complained or had a bad word to say about anyone, but I know there were occasions when things really hurt him, particularly in the world of football, which gave him some dark times, although he kept most of these feelings to himself.

John was always happy to turn his hand to anything. He loved a drink, a day at the races, working in the garden, and when his dementia sadly set in, he enjoyed many happy hours of Mindful Colouring. He loved singers Buddy Holly and John Denver, *Top Gun* and *Dirty Dancing* were his favourite films, *Phantom of the Opera* and *Les Miserables* topped his musical list and he was a whizz at mental arithmetic.

Our friends loved his sense of fun and his way of coming out with the unexpected. He was a wonderful, caring son, particularly to his mum after his dad's death, and would always go the extra mile both for her and for many others, often at the expense of himself. John could be stubborn and infuriating at times too – but can't we all!

We married in December 2005 at The Gatehouse, Edinburgh Castle. It was a truly magical day and I have been so lucky to have enjoyed 17 years as John's wife. He dealt with both his dementia and lung condition much the same way he dealt with life … he just got on with it.

Even in recent years, there would occasionally be a knock on the door or a letter through the post requesting an autograph. John was always puzzled by this, saying: 'But that was years ago, why would anyone want my autograph?' So typical of John Albert Sainty; no swagger, no side, yet his football career of over 40 years speaks for itself.

I am extremely proud of everything he achieved in life and of the way he influenced many of the contributors to this book.

I cannot thank them enough for the incredibly kind messages, which have meant so much.

I will remember John each and every day, as will his family and friends, often with a tear but always with a smile, and I will love him to the end of my days.

Finally, I received this message from Jan Bergara, Danny's widow:

'You must miss him terribly but so many wonderful memories of a life well lived and fulfilled. You have now joined the Widows' Club of two very special people who will always be in our hearts. God bless them and until we meet again.'

Lindsay

MY CHANCE TO MEET A BOYHOOD HERO

IT WAS a great pleasure for me to receive that call from Lindsay just prior to John's 70th birthday and to subsequently meet them both soon afterwards. You see, John was one of my boyhood heroes and part of the Cherries team that won promotion from the Fourth Division in 1971. It was a time when the sleepy seaside resort of Bournemouth suddenly came alive in a football sense, with its team under the flamboyant management of John Bond and possessing the prolific goalscoring ability of Ted MacDougall.

John Sainty made a considerable contribution to that promotion success, even if most of the plaudits were directed elsewhere, the first of many occasions this would happen during his career. Unfortunately, by 1975, Bond, MacDougall and 'The Saint' had all moved on and the Cherries were heading back to the Fourth Division, but what exciting times they had provided in the meantime. For a young supporter, these were seasons I would never forget.

Move the clock forward some 40 years and I found myself as club secretary of AFC Bournemouth and you can imagine how thrilled I was to welcome John back to Dean Court. As well as playing a significant part in our club's history, he had, of course, gone on to enjoy a wonderful coaching career after his playing days were over and I was delighted to at last get the chance to meet him.

I was sorry to hear that John was suffering from the early stages of Alzheimer's disease, but glimpses of his character and personality were still there, as was his dry sense of humour! He explained that he had hoped one day to come out of the shadows and write his life story. I could see from the notes that he and Lindsay handed me that information and stories had been carefully documented to cover the different stages of his life and career. He didn't say so, of course, but it also quickly became clear to me how thrilled he would be if his story could perhaps one day appear in print.

I was pleased and honoured when asked if I would help John achieve this ambition and, of course, I offered my assistance without hesitation. I looked forward to finding out more about his life and career and the opportunity to spend more time in his company. John and Lindsay were also able to accept the club's invitation to attend several matches and events at the Vitality Stadium as we progressed with the draft, including a 50th anniversary reunion dinner for members of the 1970/71 team in 2021.

Sadly, John's unexpected early passing came before we could complete the book but, with the help of others, it has been my privilege to since do so on his behalf. I have added some detail in places, but the main text contains the words and thoughts of John himself.

I could not have completed my task without Lindsay's wonderful dedication to the project and she also deserves much credit for contacting the friends, colleagues and members of John's family who have also contributed within the pages that follow. I would also like to add my thanks to them and to everyone at Pitch Publishing for their support. I hope that we have done justice to John and that the boy from Poplar would have been pleased with the end result.

Neil Vacher

MY DAD

TODAY, IF you Google Justin Fashanu's goal for Norwich against Liverpool on 9 January 1980, not only will you see a spectacular goal from a man who used to babysit me, you will also see a man in a canary yellow tracksuit celebrating in the dugout.

That man is my dad, John Sainty, and that small dugout is the first place I remember sitting and watching a game of football with him. He was one of three Johns present in the dugout that day; there was also John Bond and John Benson, together with one substitute player.

We were not sitting on luxury heated car seats as they do in the Premier League nowadays but on a hard wooden bench, with the fans inches behind us, sometimes banging on the roof of the dugout in joy and sometimes in despair.

My time in the dugout was a short-lived affair though, as I had managed to pick up some choice language from the three Johns that a young boy in the 1970s should not be repeating to his mum, Christine.

From the dugouts across the country to the benches of Wembley for the Centenary FA Cup Final in 1981, my dad sat in plenty of them. I may have only sat in one dugout with him, but I am so proud I grew up with my dad as my hero.

Mark

MY DAD

WHEN PEOPLE hear what my dad, John Sainty, achieved in his lifetime, it always makes me smile and think about what drove him to stay so focused and yet be so humble about his life experiences. Not many people get an England cap at any level or the opportunity to be a professional player, coach and manager in the game that they love so much.

He had a very selfless soul and a simplistic overview of life. From my upbringing, we saw an abundance of kindness and selflessness in everything he did. When we lived in Norwich, our home was like a conveyor belt of footballers lodging with us because, in those days, it wasn't five-star hotels when they first joined a club.

Our house became the Airbnb of its time where players stayed when they were waiting to sign for the club. We even had Justin Fashanu stay at ours for a while, as Dad had scouted him for Norwich City in the late 1970s.

My brother Mark and I grew up with footballers in all aspects of our everyday life and embraced Dad's passion for all things football. Mum, I think, was a reluctant WAG and, apart from having to be interviewed by Jimmy Tarbuck at the 1981 FA Cup Final, she shied away from all the fuss and limelight.

Mum and Dad were amazing parents. Mum laid the foundations for me to be who I am today whilst Dad brought all the experiences and chaos that he liked to create on his epic life journey. But he always put his family first and got me out of every sticky situation you could imagine – and there were plenty. His relentless energy to push himself to succeed opened up so many incredible opportunities and happy memories for us as a family.

It is almost surreal to think about what we experienced as kids growing up. Dad even brought the FA Cup home once, casually bringing it through the door as if it had just fallen off the back of a lorry for us to have a few photos with. As kids, Dad would often take Mark and I to horse racing at Newmarket or greyhounds at Great Yarmouth. We always said he was William Hill's best customer and having a cheeky bet was absolutely his guilty pleasure.

My dad was so funny, very caring and always made the time to be there for me. His quirky spontaneity often meant we had to think on our feet. He used to bring greyhounds back from Great Yarmouth. One was aptly named Sir Arthur after the Norwich chairman and he said it was destiny to bring it home! He surrounded us with love, positivity and the best amount of craziness a kid needed in life.

There are so many stories to tell. Dad's sense of fun and sometimes inappropriateness made him the perfect dad in every way. I always put him on a pedestal; he was incredible, typically embarrassing, but very much loved just the way he was.

Joanna

1
FIRST STEPS

WHO WOULD have thought that a boy from Poplar in London's East End would one day have the privilege of playing, training and coaching football alongside so many great legends in the game, of being involved in some magical moments, travelling to amazing countries and working with the truly memorable Danny Bergara, one of the first international coaches/managers to be appointed in England. But I am getting ahead of myself, so here is where it all began.

I was born in Bow Hospital, East London to Mum, Lilias, and Dad, Bert, on 24 March 1946 and my first home was a flat in Poplar, which we shared with my 'Little Nan', her sister, Aunt 'Tilly Whip', and my mother's two brothers, Albert and Bertie. It was all very crowded, but no one ever complained. Just like the opening scene in the BBC TV series *Call the Midwife*, I remember the view from our back window was often dominated by the sight of a large ship in dock, the size of which seemed to overshadow all the other buildings in the area.

From Monday to Friday, Dad would cycle to work in East India Docks. Uncle Bertie also worked in the docks, whilst Uncle Albert was a barge builder on the Thames. Bertie had a habit of bringing all sorts of goodies home because his philosophy was 'if it's not screwed down take it, if it is, find a screwdriver!' He was a loveable rogue.

A very important item in the household was my dad's docker's hook. This item was precious as, without it, Dad could not work. I remember it well, a light, coloured wooden handle, a little longer in length than a man's hand with an S-shaped hook hanging below to enable you to grab the bales from the holds of the ship. Dad kept the hook hanging from a belt around his waist and it was certainly not to be tampered with.

Life was not always easy for my parents as they were both extremely hard-working. Dad had to make sure he arrived early for work each day as the amount of work available depended on how many ships were in dock and how many men were needed to unload them. It paid to try to get as near to the front of the queue as possible because those not required were sent home without pay. Fortunately, I don't have too many memories of him returning home early, but it was always a relief to set off for school without seeing him return.

I remember every Sunday the 'Winkle Man' would call round. So, winkles for tea, which I loved, and many a Sunday evening we would sit round and play cards. My dad always loved to cheat! My only pet as a kid was a budgerigar we called 'Cocky'; he lived a long time as far as I remember, although I was always frightened that he might escape and fly away.

When I was around seven years of age, we moved to a prefab in Dagenham, Essex. Mum got a job in a local factory which made doors, but Dad now had a much longer journey to work and bought a Lambretta scooter, quite the rage then, and a small car, which he would only use on the weekend. I would never miss an opportunity to take the Lambretta out if I could get away with it and the crash helmet I wore was a perfect disguise; bearing in mind that I was big for my age, I could get away with looking as though I was legally old enough to drive. Prior to having the car, as Mum and Dad worked Monday to Friday, our weekend routine would most often be the same. If I was lucky, I would be given two shillings to go to Saturday morning pictures instead of going shopping with Mum. I used to catch a bus to the cinema but craftily would walk back to Nan's using my return bus fare to buy chips. Another vivid memory of a Saturday morning was shopping in Crisp Street, well known in the East End, and buying pie and mash at the famous shop, Tubby Isaacs. That was not to be missed. For, as well as pie and mash, it was locally famed for jellied eels, which were delicious with plenty of vinegar and pepper. I still love both to this day.

Saturday afternoons saw us all take the trolley bus back to Poplar, having picked up some shopping for 'Little Nan' – she was less than 5ft tall, so hence the nickname – to return to the flat we left when I was small and where Nan and her siblings continued to live.

My dad's parents lived in Rainham, Essex and often visited us on Sundays, although sometimes Dad and I cycled the 14-mile round trip to go and see them.

It was Dad who initially wanted me to be a professional footballer, probably more than I did, and by the time I had reached five or six years old, he had already mapped out my career. I think he really hoped I would take a different path to working in the docks. At every opportunity he would take me over to the local park where we would kick the ball to each other for what seemed like hours on end. Dad never seemed to get fed up whereas I was always asking 'Can we go home now?

Is tea ready?' But it was always Dad's decision when the session was to end.

I remember how Dad would kick the ball in all directions and sometimes he would point in one direction and see if I anticipated correctly and, if I did, he would often change direction so that I would have to go the other way and end up running three times as far as I originally intended. No wonder I often got fed up; only one of us was enjoying the session and it definitely wasn't me!

My first taste of professional football came when Dad took me to watch West Ham at Upton Park. We went to most of their Football League games. I think I would have been about seven years old and I remember the crowd would pass the kids down towards the front or sometimes, if we were late getting there, I remember being passed along towards the corner by the goal and tied on to the side posts of the surrounding fence for safety! How times change.

Dad was also very keen on tennis and, when we weren't playing or watching football, we would be out on the tennis court. I loved tennis and I became quite a handy player as a result, good enough to seriously consider taking it up instead of football a few years later. Apart from that, though, it was pretty much football all year round, even during our summer holidays when my parents regularly took me a few miles up the road to Seacroft Holiday Camp at Hemsby on Sea, near Great Yarmouth. Every Friday, there was a monumental football match against Hemsby Holiday Camp, which was situated 200 yards down the road. The game was always at their place because they had a better pitch and the whole camp would march in procession down the road with the football team at the head of the column. The rivalry between the two camps was unbelievable and these games were uncompromising battles, but I am pleased to say my record was played five, won five.

I was always big as a youngster, perfect for a centre-half, and to begin with nobody would believe that I was only 12 years old, as I was already 5ft 6in tall. I still had to get my dad's permission to join in and play but prior to Friday's game there would be a series of trial games during the week at the respective camps to select the teams. Dad fancied himself as a bit of a player and would always play in these trial games. One year we were on opposing sides and when we tackled each other for the ball, the outcome was that Dad broke two ribs, which more or less put paid to his football career. Not a nice way to end a holiday but in Dad's eyes I could do no wrong on the football field, although he could occasionally be my greatest critic. He still found time to clean my boots and whiten my laces every week, though.

I enjoyed playing a variety of athletics and sports at school and soon became joint intermediate high jump champion, perhaps unsurprisingly given my height. My early football teachers were Mr Perryman at Campbell Middle School, Mr Winter at S.E.E. County Technical School and Mr Otigari at Barking District School. In all honesty, they didn't teach me very much about the game. Most of the time they would pick two teams and play an 11-a-side game for an hour. Norman Otigari also ran our local district team and we did train on a Friday night in the school gym, mostly physical exercises for half an hour before playing three-a-side for the second half an hour ahead of our game the following morning.

By the time I reached 12 years of age, I was already playing for Barking Boys under-13s, although I was actually in the under-12 age group. One day, Dad saw a man called Dicky Walker watching one of our games from the touchline. Dicky had played professionally for West Ham, the team Dad supported, and he approached Dicky to ask if I could have a trial for the Hammers. Dad was disappointed when he said no, but the blow was slightly softened when he said I could have one with Tottenham Hotspur, as Dicky was by now working for them and not West Ham!

So, every school holiday, off I went to Spurs for some 'proper training' along with two other lads who played in the same Barking team. The Embery twins, William and Benjamin, affectionately known as Bill and Ben, were a year older but they always looked after me. I was extremely fortunate and privileged to have this opportunity at such a young age.

To get to White Hart Lane we had to first take a train to Barking, then another to South Tottenham before catching a bus or walking 20 minutes to reach the ground. We often walked if we had time to save the bus fare that we could claim as part of our expenses at the end of the week. Once we were there, we would be encouraged to practise our ball control and passing; one of the sayings that used to filter through at Tottenham was 'Can't pass, can't play.' These early training sessions consisted of playing the ball for hours, drilling it against the high brick wall that surrounded the car park, where the players and directors parked their big cars on matchdays. But it wasn't all about fun and playing football, we were also expected to help with other tasks around the ground and spent many an hour giving the railings on the terraces a fresh coat of paint.

At schoolboy level, I was playing between 60 and 80 games a season, usually at right half-back. I like to think I modelled myself on Tottenham and Northern Ireland defender Danny Blanchflower and, according to the local press at the time, I was one of the 'youngsters to watch'. In the opinion of reporter Willie Evans, the Barking and Dagenham area that had previously unearthed England internationals Jimmy Greaves and Terry Venables now had 'some other good 'uns coming along, including Dagenham centre-forward Tom Mcleod and inside-right Jimmy Scott, and another youngster you are sure to hear about – right-half John Sainty, the Barking captain, who is bound to get county honours'.

Nonetheless, any delusions I may have had about being an automatic selection for Barking were quashed after I failed to report for training the day before an English Schools' Trophy tie against Southend at Mayesbrook Park. Mr Otagiri decided that disciplinary action was required and, after taking a vote amongst my team-mates, I was suspended. The boys decided that if I could not be bothered to turn up for training, then I could not expect to play. Deservedly, I was made to sit in the stand and left to think about what I had done while watching Southend win 3-2.

We played in the Corinthian League and on occasions the opposition was not always that strong and I remember how, in the first game after my suspension, we sailed to an easy 10-0 victory against Barnes and Richmond. I was so delighted to be back playing, I scored a hat-trick. The game was watched by Terence Hopley of the *Dagenham Post* who reported: 'Technical schoolboy John Sainty was undoubtedly the most powerful player on the field and yet he was the only one trying in the closing stages. But even he felt sorry for Barnes and blurted out a spontaneous "well done son" to the little full-back who was lucky enough to beat him on one occasion!'

I was certainly strongly built for my age and my first taste of higher grade football came when I was 13 years old and was selected for the London Schools under-15 team to play Ebbw Vale. This was a big step up in age range for me and it seemed a different world travelling down to Wales by coach and staying in a hotel. Ronnie Harris, who had just signed for Chelsea, was also in the team and it's where I first met Alan Dennis, our captain, who later became my youth-team captain at Tottenham Hotspur. Alan was always immaculately turned out as if he had just stepped out of Burton's shop window! He even managed to avoid getting any mud splattered on his lilywhite Spurs shirt!

The following year, 1961, I captained Barking, Essex and London Schools. The best game we had was against a very strong Manchester Schools team, who were regarded as the cream of English football. Most of their players had already signed for one of the Manchester or Liverpool clubs and the game should have been played at White Hart Lane. However, because the pitch was unfit, it was staged at Spurs' Cheshunt training ground and we were brilliant that day, winning by something like ten goals to four.

After that game, I received a call-up as a travelling reserve for the England Schoolboy trials at Derby and eventually played in the second half of a game for the Rest against England. I must have done well as, four days later, Dicky Walker called round to our house and informed my parents that I had been selected to play at centre-half for the actual England Schools starting XI in their forthcoming match against Wales at Swansea. I would be following in the footsteps of another Barking boy, John O'Rourke, who, although a year older, was a good mate of mine and had been picked for the England side the previous year. Much later, we would become team-mates at Bournemouth.

The England party stayed in a hotel on the Mumbles and we beat Wales out of sight, 7-3, with John Sissons scoring a hat-trick. Mum and Dad were amongst the crowd of 10,000 at Vetch Field and I remember one of the press quotes after the game stated that 'Sainty's clever play helped to achieve the England's win'. My other main recollection of that trip is of our midfielder Trevor Dawkins sitting up in bed most of the night wearing his England cap and still having it on his head when he woke up in the morning! Of my team-mates for that game, John and Trevor were bound for West Ham along with Martin Britt, while Glyn Pardoe and Alan Ogley went to Manchester City, Howard Kendall to Preston and Peter Storey to Spurs' London rivals, Arsenal.

From there, it was a game for London Boys against Birmingham at Selhurst Park where the result was a 10-1 thrashing for an out-of-touch Birmingham side, in which I scored the seventh and tenth goals. I was then chosen to fly with a party of 15 lads to Hamburg for the England v Germany Schoolboy international in Hagen, but I did not make the starting XI and was also a reserve for the England v Eire international at Coventry.

Unfortunately, my England career did not progress beyond this, but it was good while it lasted. Possibly, being big was not so good now.

On the educational front, I was one of only four lads in my year at Campbell Middle School who passed the 13-plus exam. Of the other three, one was the headmaster's son, where a bit of nepotism may have crept in, and another one was a boy the head wanted to get rid of! As a result, I moved on to a new school, South-East Essex County Technical High, which proved to be quite a mouthful whenever I mentioned it on numerous future CVs.

Educationally, I hated the place. I was supposed to make up two years, as all the other pupils in my class had been there since they passed their 11-plus exams. It was deemed that, academically, I was a late developer but, by the time I started there, I was almost certain that I was going to be offered an apprenticeship at Spurs, so unless the lesson was PE or some other sport, I was not that interested.

The school had a brilliant system in place which allowed you to 'sign out' if you had to go somewhere like the doctor or dentist during school time. I signed myself out of most lessons but not necessarily for these reasons – and got caught out a couple of times – but on my 15th birthday the school decided that, at my father's request and as I had a job to go to, I could leave a year early. I was on my way to Spurs.

2

JOURNEY TO THE STARS

SO, IN 1961, at 15 years of age, I joined Tottenham Hotspur as an apprentice footballer.

That was the job title in those days, not YTS or academy scholar, and as an apprentice I learned to clean boots, wash and scrub bathrooms and toilets, sweep the gym, stack and tidy the weights room, sweep the terraces and help the groundsman with the pitch in winter – either clearing the snow or helping manoeuvre the giant plastic covers used to protect the pitch. There was training twice a day Monday to Thursday, whilst Friday was spent doing light training but was heavy on chores in preparation for matchday on Saturday.

My youth-team coach/trainer was Johnny Wallace, who was responsible for the apprentices, whilst Jack Coxford looked after the reserves and Cecil Poynton the first team alongside manager Bill Nicholson. Johnny, Jack and Cecil all invariably wore white coats because they doubled up as physiotherapists and fitness trainers, each looking after their own squads. Sid Tickridge sometimes helped Johnny to coach the youth-team and every Tuesday and Thursday an Olympic weightlifter by the name of Bill Watson would work with all the players in the various squads to improve their strength and agility.

My first day as an apprentice was one that I would never forget, travelling by train from my Dagenham prefab alongside the city workers to do a job that thousands could only dream of. I was so excited to start my soccer career with all those famous names like Danny Blanchflower, Jimmy Greaves, Cliff Jones and Dave Mackay.

There was no slacking on the first day. We trained at Cheshunt and I was lucky enough to get a lift from White Hart Lane to Cheshunt from first-team player Terry Dyson. Loosening-up exercises, ball control, sprints and a cross country run followed. That was the programme. Club captain Blanchflower won the race … I came last! I never had so many aches and pains from training, but I knew I would have to lose a bit of weight, as I was 13st and needed to get down to 12. After about three weeks of a tough training regime, I had done exactly that and lost the stone I had set out to.

There was a tremendous atmosphere at training. The apprentices worked alongside the stars who took Spurs to the Football League and FA Cup double the previous year; there were no privileged individuals and everyone worked together. I remember sessions in the gym often involved a lot of weight training taken by Bill Watson and we also did agility work, jumping through hoops and on to benches, all different and enjoyable until we came to the dreaded rope.

We had to climb this rope which was attached to the roof about 30ft above our heads. Getting up was an effort, but coming down was harder, as most of your energy had been used going up. You had to use as much energy to get back down and if you tried to slide down, you would burn your hands. So, we had to make a decision, drop 30ft or burn our hands!

Another routine exercise involved hanging a ball on a rope from the ceiling of the gym; we had to swing from side to side before timing our jumps to ensure we made contact with the ball. Heading practice involved using a medicine ball in pairs, standing six to eight feet apart. One would throw the ball underarm to his partner, who would attempt to head it back. This was supposed to strengthen the neck muscles but more often than not made us see stars.

As well as the first team, reserve and youth teams, Spurs fielded a mixed age team in the Metropolitan League and this was used as a bridge between the youth-team and the reserves. The club also ran an under-16/under-18 team in the Wood Green League, mainly for amateur players and trialists, and in charge of this team was a real gentleman called Jimmy Joyce who, although only 5ft 4in tall, was twice as big in circumference!

Jim was someone you could always turn to and he also worked in the club's ticket office during the week, as well as being responsible for paying out the players' expenses. He normally trusted that you had asked for the correct amount but if he didn't believe you for any reason, he would give you a terribly frightening look, plenty enough to make you ensure you got your expenses right the next time!

At the end of every season, Jimmy would organise a trip abroad to enable us to take part in a youth tournament – always in the Netherlands. We would take a train from Liverpool Street to Harwich, then a ferry from Harwich to the Hook of Holland and finally a coach on to our destination.

I used to love the footballing side of these trips, playing against top European youth teams, but not so much the accommodation, which was arranged with local host families.

The people were lovely and couldn't do enough for you, but I invariably ended up on my own miles from anywhere instead of being with team-mates.

The tournaments we played in took us to different clubs in the Netherlands such as Feyenoord, Ajax, Groningen and PSV Eindhoven, and gave us an insight into the way football was structured there from an early age. They all had the same set-up with a main stadium, training ground with numerous training pitches, a large clubhouse with good facilities and numerous football teams from nine to 18 years old, then under-21, reserves and first team.

The players trained and played there from a young age as there was no schools football in the Netherlands. Each team had its own manager, coach and physio who worked on players strengths and weaknesses, while games took place against sides of the same age range from other clubs. Most importantly, these opportunities were available to large numbers of youngsters, unlike in England where at an early age you were, more often than not, taught how to play football by an English or mathematics teacher who picked two teams of *x* number a side and played 30 minutes each way, with the big boys dictating and the little ones lucky to get a touch of the ball.

It was only the lucky ones who were spotted by a scout from one of the professional clubs and had the privilege of receiving any kind of organised and structured training. I was one of the lucky ones. I was privileged.

In this country, it took us some 20 to 25 years to catch up with the top continentals and legalise the training of our young and aspiring footballers by introducing schools of excellence and eventually the academy system. The only problem that still remains is that, if you look closely at the set-up for many academies and schools of excellence, there are still a large percentage of present or former schoolteachers involved. Although I may not have realised it at the time, the value of the system I witnessed in Holland as a young player would stay with me throughout my professional career and later I would have the opportunity to put these processes into operation in my future roles in coaching and as an academy director.

As an apprentice at Spurs, you worked in large groups, but the training was structured around playing lots of games. We played on Saturdays in the South-East Counties League, which was against players of our own age, and in midweek we played in the Metropolitan League, which was open-aged and sometimes quite physical. Although you had teams of a similar stature like Arsenal, West Ham and Chelsea in the Metropolitan League, others included Wisbech, March Town, Bury St Edmunds and the Metropolitan Police, who definitely did not take any prisoners. With the mixture of games, you grew up quickly as a 17 or 18-year-old.

Although I was not particularly tall, just under 5ft 10in, I had been used to playing in the centre of defence, but in those days Spurs played with only one centre-half, so they tried me out in different positions. First it was full-back, then in midfield, but eventually I ended up playing centre-forward, in the Bobby Smith mould, rather than like Alan Gilzean. I took to it like a duck to water and, because of the large number of games I played in during one season as an eighteen-year-old, I scored plenty of goals and eventually became the leading goalscorer for our 'A' team, although unfortunately I had to 'lose' four of my Met goals against Barnet Reserves when they resigned from the League.I also remember being dropped on one occasion for a game against Southend United because I had missed training, choosing to watch my girlfriend Christine in a swimming competition instead. This was not something I would ever repeat. The game saw me sitting in the stand at Mayesbrook Arena in the company of Spurs scout, Dick Walker. We lost the match 3-2 but I was back in the side in the Corinthian League the following week, playing against Barnes & Richmond. We won 10-0 and I scored a hat-trick. The goals kept flowing – I was averaging a goal a game in the 'A' team – but still I was considered too raw and inexperienced to play regularly in the reserves or come close to breaking into the first-team set-up. It was not surprising really as, after becoming only the third English club to achieve a domestic league and cup double, Bill Nicholson's side had gone on to retain the FA Cup in 1962 and win the European Cup Winners' Cup the following year. In the European final, held in Rotterdam, they thrashed the holders, Atlético Madrid, 5-1 with two goals apiece from Greaves and Dyson, and another from John White.

In the league, they had followed up their 1961 championship success by finishing third, second and fourth in the three seasons that immediately followed. Nicholson was joined by former Spurs and England inside-forward Eddie Baily, who was appointed assistant manager in 1963. But, in July 1964, the club suffered a devastating blow. The tragic death of Scottish international midfielder John White at the age of just 27 shocked us all. White was tragically killed by a lightning strike while sheltering under a tree during a thunderstorm at Crews Hill golf course in Enfield.

John possessed a combination of skills and played a significant part in the club's success after joining from Falkirk in 1959. As well as regularly chipping in with goals himself, his passing and ball control helped sustain the team's attacking momentum, while his runs to find space off the ball became legendary. He would arrive unexpectedly and unnoticed in the opposition's penalty area and the White Hart Lane faithful soon nicknamed him 'The Ghost'.

Returning to matters closer to home at the time, as well as playing and training, all the youngsters were expected to get involved in other aspects of the club and I was always willing to take on anything and give it a try. I was chosen to help out in the club offices on Friday afternoons, this being the busiest time of the week as everyone prepared for Saturday's game. Our coach, Johnny Wallace, did not think much of this, as he thought I was skiving, so he made sure that during the rest of the week I did my share of cleaning in the dressing rooms and the gym and he made a particular point of carefully inspecting my work, so I had to make sure I did everything meticulously.

Spurs also encouraged all their apprentices to take their Preliminary Coaching Badge and this meant travelling to Arsenal's Highbury Stadium every Monday afternoon. I thoroughly enjoyed this and successfully gained my badge. Then, together with team-mate Roger Hoy, I took the Spurs schoolboy players in training on three nights each week and I also attended a trainers' course for the treatment of injuries and coached boys at East Ham Secondary School and Barking under-13s. How valuable all this would prove to be in my later career. Although I was only 18 myself, I loved coaching the kids, three of whom spring to mind – Steve Perryman, Phil Holder and Ray Clarke, who all went on to play in the Spurs first team.

As much as I enjoyed coaching the club's youngsters, I could not understand why Spurs had no coaches in place to take the schoolboys. Roger and I were only two or three years older than them. Nowadays, clubs would have any number of schoolboy coaches.

Unfortunately, though, it was not just my coaching and ability on the pitch that eventually came to Mr Nicholson's attention, as word reached him that I had got myself involved with some of the players who liked a bet. One of the professionals had said he was going to do a Tote double, which I had no idea about at that time, and he said if I gave him ten shillings, he would place a bet for me alongside his. The next day, he gave me my winnings of £5, which was equivalent to a whole week's wages, so this naturally inflamed my interest. So, my next bet came at the start of the flat racing season and I did what was called a 'spring double', picking out the Lincoln winner on the Wednesday and then betting on the following Saturday's Grand National steeplechase. My selection was Old Tom in the Lincoln and the horse won. My choice for the National was Jay Trump and I remember playing that afternoon for the 'A' team at the Cheshunt training ground and, as we approached half-time, I knew my horse had won because my dad, who used to watch all my games, was jumping up and down on the touchline like a lunatic! I had won £130 on the two bets, but it was the start of a slippery slope and from there I joined the betting group among the apprentices.

Our group would visit greyhound tracks at Walthamstow, White City, Park Royal and Dagenham, plus several horse racing tracks that were all within easy reach such as Ascot, Kempton, Lingfield and Sandown Park. This was only a spare time activity, because we did not do extra training at that time, only working in the mornings. With plenty of free afternoons to fill, we had to find somewhere to go and something to do and, unfortunately, we fell into bad habits.

One day, I came home and immediately sensed that something was wrong. Dad had received a call from Mr Nicholson, who was concerned about the company I had fallen in with and had asked Dad to have a strong word with me. I promised I would give up the gambling, although I did fall back into it some while later.

Although I signed professional forms for the club in 1963, it was not until the 1965/66 season that I was selected regularly for the reserve team. After scoring 14 goals in six games for the 'A' team, I got a chance in the reserves, where I seemed to go from strength to strength as Tottenham challenged for honours in the Football Combination. I was again likened to the former Spurs double winner and England forward Bobby Smith, possibly because I was also a well-built, bustling type of player who believed that the basic philosophy of football was essentially uncomplicated – bang the ball into the opposition's goal as frequently as possible.

I was lucky enough to score 55 goals in 41 games the following season, including 31 in 39 games for the reserve team which won the Combination League, and another 24 in just nine games for the 'A' side. Amongst my team-mates during that successful season were other young players such as Dennis Bond, Peter Collins, Roger Hoy, Jimmy Pearce, Derek Posse, John Pratt, Tony Want and Keith Weller. Despite my success at reserve-team level, however, I was no nearer to stepping into the first team.

The first team had not won any silverware since their European success in 1963 and had gradually slipped down the First Division table, finishing sixth in 1964/65 and eight in 1965/66. Not a dramatic decline, but not enough to match the expectations of the club and its supporters. The 1966/67 saw a slight improvement, with Spurs eventually finishing third after challenging eventual champions Manchester United and surprise runners-up Nottingham Forest throughout the season. However, towards the end of that campaign, there was a clamour amongst supporters and in the local media for me to be given a chance in the first team.

There were numerous letters in the press from fans and columnist Lou Margetts wrote in the Spurs match programme: 'Fielding the most expensive first team in the history of British football, this Spurs side has undoubted talent, but its brittle performance is failing where it counts most – it can only score goals the hard way and it isn't scoring anything like enough.' He went on to suggest that 'Jimmy Greaves had lost his edge, and the hard and direct approach of Frank Saul and John Sainty would blend better with the subtlety of [Alan] Gilzean and the industry of [Terry] Venables'. They were fantastic words for me to read and there were many more praising my good positional sense, sure shot and knowledge of where the goal was.

To have broken into the first team for just one game would have been the most treasured memory of my career, but the squad at the time consisted of the likes of Bill Brown, Pat Jennings, Ron Henry, Cyril Knowles, Frank Saul, Maurice Norman, Alan Mullery, Alan Gilzean, Cliff Jones, Jimmy Robertson, Jimmy Greaves, Terry Venables and my greatest hero of all-time, Dave Mackay. I made sure that I was the one who got to clean the great man's boots whilst serving my apprenticeship.

Dave was a brilliant footballer, but his favourite trick was to show you how to toss a coin into the air, then catch it on his forehead and drop it into his top pocket. Although it was your coin that you had lent him to show everyone the trick, funnily enough you never saw it again! I was Dave's boot boy until I signed professional forms at 17. By then, you were no longer expected to do the chores like boot cleaning and kit preparation. It meant I didn't have to turn up early at White Hart Lane, so I would often catch a bus from home to Gants Hill, where I was lucky enough to be picked up by either Terry Venables or Frank Saul in their cars and driven on to the training ground at Cheshunt.

But a chance to prove myself in the first team never came and I seemed to be moving further down the pecking order at White Hart Lane. Watching some of my younger team-mates getting opportunities, I started to question my own ability. Other youngsters of my era did also eventually break into the first team such as Phil Beal, John Pratt, Jimmy Pearce, Derek Possee and Keith Weller. At first, Keith and I did not get on at all; we both wanted to be 'cock of the walk' and this resulted in a scrap during a training session in the gym. It seemed to clear the air and, from that day, we became the best of friends, always meeting up at weekends. Eventually, Keith was best man at my wedding. I returned the favour at his wedding and for some reason even went on the honeymoon with him and his wife to Majorca!

I also remember Neil Johnston breaking into the first team. No disrespect to Neil but as a winger his greatest attribute was that he could run all day at quite a quick pace and at the end of the season we used to say that Neil was going in for a 100,000-mile service while the rest of us were going to enjoy our end-of-season break! Neil made 34 appearances and although these were spread across six years, the five goals he scored would mean a lot more to him now than my 55 at a more inferior level.

The only time I shared a pitch with the first team was if they wanted to use us reserves as cannon fodder and played against us in training. On these occasions, Mike England used to kick seven bells out of me. I had been associated with Spurs since I was 12 years old and had left school one year early to be an apprentice professional at the age of 15, signing professional forms at 17. Now, at 21 and shortly to be married, my career seemed to be going nowhere. I even asked my dad to find out about a job in the docks with him, as entry in those days could be passed along from father to son.

Nonetheless, on 27 May 1967, I married my girlfriend, Christine Bradford. We had originally met whilst both attending South-East Essex County Technical High School and had been courting for five years or so. We couldn't afford a home of our own, so we lived with my parents at the prefab in Dagenham. Marriage brought me down to earth and I soon realised I now had responsibilities, and this encouraged me to behave myself.

The previous week, Spurs had won the FA Cup, beating London rivals Chelsea 2-1, but as the first-team group trained separately to us youngsters, I did not experience much of the build-up to the big day at Wembley. We were taken by coach to see the match itself but we returned directly to the ground afterwards and did not get invited to any of the post-match celebrations. Our second goal that day was scored by winger Frank Saul, another of the players whose boots it had been my job to clean during my apprenticeship.

Eventually, I was offered a further one-year contract during the summer of 1967, but Mr Nicholson said he could make me no promises beyond that and hinted I may find myself in the same position in another 12 months' time.

It was a no-brainer really and time for me to move on.

In the words of Terry Dyson

'John Sainty was all right as a bloke. He used to mix in well with all us players. I played with him a few times and he was a goalscoring centre-forward. Used to score regularly. A fair player, but he never really got a chance in the first team.

'Spurs were doing so well with what is said to be the greatest team in their history when he was coming through. We were a good team. And John had Bobby Smith, an England international, as a direct rival for the No.9 shirt. It was difficult to get him in.

'A shame really, because otherwise John might have made it, but he went on to play for Reading and Bournemouth and coached Manchester City when Spurs beat them in the 1981 FA Cup Final, so he got a living out of the game.'

Terry Dyson was a Tottenham clubmate of John's and part of the Spurs side which became the first team in the 20th century to complete the League and FA Cup double in 1961, his goal against Leicester City in the knockout decider at Wembley sealing the feat. Dyson was also player-of-the-match as the Lilywhites became the first British side to lift a major European club trophy, netting two goals in the 5-1 European Cup Winners' Cup Final win over Atlético Madrid in Rotterdam two years later.

In the words of Mike Donovan

'I first recall John Sainty when he wore the centre-forward shirt for Tottenham Hotspur's Football Combination side in 1963. I had given my football heart to the club two years earlier.

'My dad – with my mum – had followed the club since Arthur Rowe led the club's 'push and run' team to back-to-back titles in 1949/50 and 1950/51. He never pushed me into becoming a Spurs fan, whizzing me around London to also see the likes of Fulham, Brentford and Leyton Orient. But when he eventually took me to White Hart Lane to see Spurs for the first time it was love at first sight after climbing the flight of steps on to the Lane's East Stand terraces and viewing the green sward of a pitch and the packed crowd.

'Spurs were the team of the moment, having become the first in the 20th century to secure the double of First Division title and the FA Cup in the same season. It could be argued they were the best club side worldwide because of the entertaining, skilled, thrilling way manager Bill Nicholson had got them playing to create history. And they went on to retain the FA Cup the following season and become the first British team to claim a major European club trophy by lifting the Cup Winners' Cup a year later.

'I couldn't get enough of them, which is why we also attended the Combination games played at the ground on alternate Saturdays to the first team. John Sainty was a regular in Spurs' second string and, in my memory, wore a number nine on the back of his solid frame and scored hatsful of goals, although he modestly told me once, "There were a lot of good players around me. It made my job easy".' His efforts would probably have earned him a place in the first team at most other clubs, but Spurs were blessed with an unmatched depth of quality and also had the good fortune of having starters who were rarely injured. For instance, in contrast to today's mega squads, Spurs completed the glory road to the double in 1960/61 with just 17 players.

'It all meant John never got a look-in. For starters, he was understudying to Bobby Smith before Alan Gilzean, the 'King of White Hart Lane', replaced the one-time all-time Spurs record goalscorer. His path was also blocked should he have tried to muscle into other positions by the likes of the inspirational Dave Mackay, his hero and in my experience the club's greatest player, and captain extraordinaire Danny Blanchflower, as well as Cliff Jones, rated the finest of wingers. And they were just three of that glittering side of the early 1960s, the greatest era of the club's history.

'Opportunities for the reserve players were clearly few and far between, even though there were some decent performers in their side such as Tony Marchi, Welsh international Mel Hopkins, Johnny Hollowbread and, of course, John himself. He had to settle for helping the second team to a series of Football Combination titles and eventually moved away to get first-team opportunities.

'But three years before he departed for Reading in 1967, John figured in a reserve game which was of huge significance when I came to write the authorised biography of Dave Mackay (*Dave Mackay: Football's Braveheart on Pitch*). Spurs were taking on Shrewsbury Town in a Combination encounter. Mackay's left leg had been shattered in a collision with Manchester United's Noel Cantwell at Old Trafford as holders Spurs exited the European Cup Winners' Cup ten months earlier. He was on the comeback trail, which was cruelly ended this day when the same leg was broken. I wanted first-hand testimony, but we were in 2021 and knew it would be difficult to get it. That's where John came in and he was happy to share his memories, along with team-mate that day, Les Allen. I'll never forget that gesture, reflecting a lovely, giving chap.

'We had a few delightful and touching email exchanges. When he took delivery of my Mackay book he wrote: "Am in awe. So pleased to have made a small contribution but will be reading this over and over again. How lucky was I to have known and played with such a man." Strangely, I was considering sending a message to him as we dementia sufferers need to support each other.

'Later in life, I got to know John personally when reporting football matches. By then he had gone on to enjoy a fine career as a player and coach. But when our paths crossed in press boxes when he was working as a statistician, we got chatting and kept in touch.

'I was saddened to hear of his passing. I know the process of putting this book together has been a therapy for his devoted wife Lindsay. And it will ensure future generations will be able to read the story of an individual who was a football man and, more importantly, a decent man through and through. Shine on, John Albert Sydney Sainty.'

Award-winning author **Mike Donovan** has written numerous Tottenham-related books including *The King of White Hart Lane* (Alan Gilzean), *Glory, Glory Lane, Spurs' Greatest Games, Spurs' Unsung Hero* (Terry Dyson) and *Takenote!* (Darren Anderton). A Spurs fan since 1961, he has been a journalist for 40 years and has worked as a boxing and tennis correspondent and sports editor.

3

BACK DOWN TO EARTH

RATHER THAN accept Mr Nicholson's offer of a further one-year contract, I informed him that I would like a move elsewhere to forward my career. I explained it was nothing to do with money, purely about wanting first-team football and I didn't care in which division.

I was disappointed that the club then placed a transfer fee of £12,000 on my head. I believed this was excessive at the time for a player with no first-team experience and that it was likely to put off some potential suitors. I even appealed to the Football League to intervene, but they misunderstood my argument totally and refused, thinking I was unhappy with the personal terms offered to me by Tottenham.

Plymouth Argyle and Millwall showed some interest in me, but Mr Nicholson, who to my mind was still God, had a very good friend called Freddie Cox, the former Arsenal winger who was part of the Gunners' 1950 FA Cup-winning team. In the summer of 1967, Mr Cox was in his second spell as manager at Bournemouth & Boscombe Athletic and it was suggested I should go and have a chat with him regarding my future. Out of courtesy I agreed, but at the same time Reading manager Roy Bentley, the former Chelsea and England forward, also expressed an interest, so we agreed that before making any decision I would speak to both gentlemen.

I went down to talk to Mr Cox but I felt Mr Bentley was more convincing. The clubs were very similar in status, both being in the Third Division, but his stance was that Reading was much nearer to London where I had lived all my life and where my family remained. In addition, Spurs were offering me £25 per week whilst Reading's offer was £40 per week plus a £1,000 signing-on fee and they also loaned me a deposit to put down on a new £5,000 house.

Another no-brainer then. Reading it was. Mr Bentley originally offered Tottenham £8,000 for my signature and talks went on for several weeks before Reading eventually agreed to meet the £12,000 amidst further interest from Bournemouth. So, three months after they had first enquired about me, I signed for the Biscuitmen on 17 August 1967 and the fee equalled the previous club record they had paid for a player.

I imagine both managers were aware of the fee before we spoke but I honestly couldn't understand why Spurs wanted that kind of money for someone of my unproven ability and why there were these two clubs willing to pay it. Perhaps Mr Nicholson rated me more than he had let on? I must have made an impression on him as many years later, while attending a function at White Hart Lane, I will never forget the fond way he greeted and remembered me. It nearly knocked me off my feet.

Not everything was rosier at Reading than Bournemouth. For instance, when I spoke to Mr Cox, the players were training on the tarmac car park, whereas at Reading I soon found out that the players changed at the ground before going down the road to train at dog track – not round it but, in the middle! I had been to enough dog tracks to be aware of what happens in the middle section – the greyhounds relieve themselves! So, before we could commence training, the apprentices had to clear as much of the mess as they could find.

Training was hard but mainly enjoyable, apart from when we did crossing and shooting practice. If the ball came across to you at head height, you invariably ducked as nine times out of ten the ball had some elusive dog mess on it. You certainly didn't want that in your hair! The same went when picking up the ball for a throw-in – it was essential to check it first.

Sometimes we trained in the stadium at Elm Park, but this was not all good news, as we knew these sessions would last for hours. Initially, I could not work out why so many of the lads got niggly little pulls and strains towards the end of these sessions, enough to make them leave the field. I eventually realised that Mr Bentley was, in fact, the problem. During his playing career, he had been a prolific goalscorer for Chelsea, winning 12 caps for England and he loved nothing more than for hours on end having us cross the ball for him to strike at goal. To be fair, he was pretty good and he also knew that, by training at Elm Park, the balls would have nothing nasty on them!

At Spurs, very few of the lads lived near to each other, but it was different at Reading and we all met up in a café near the ground before training. A cup of tea and a laugh was usually the order of the day, plus a go on the pinball machine, with everybody wanting to be the champion and claim the highest score. We all worked hard each day in training, then returned to the café afterwards to repeat the morning routine.

I made my Football League debut in the first game of the season against Stockport County and noticed I would be up against two huge central defenders. One was Matt Woods and the other was Eddie Stuart, a player who could still give me nightmares to this day. He had been a legendary figure at Wolves during the 1950s and had taken over from former captain Billy Wright upon his retirement in 1959. A charismatic but formidable figure on the field, my initial thoughts about him were not wrong and by the end of the game I had been battered black and blue. I did, however, have the satisfaction of scoring twice in a 3-0 win and received an eight-star rating in the following morning's newspaper, so Reading fans probably thought they had the bargain of the century! 'Enter the Saint!' was the headline in the *Reading Chronicle*.

I must admit I did have some trouble adjusting to the faster pace of league football and made the mistake of starting off too quickly. I nearly seized up after the first quarter of an hour and had to take things easier to enable me to get through the rest of the game.

My goals came in the seventh and 70th minutes before Dennis Allen grabbed the third. My first goal in the Football League had a freakish look about it. After receiving a pass from Allen, I crossed from the right wing and the spinning and rising ball was deflected into the top of the net off County defender Brian Gallagher. I didn't care, I was up and running, although the local newspaper subsequently credited Gallagher with an own goal.

There was no doubt about my second, though, a close-range header from a cross by George Harris. Another debutant for Reading that day was John Collins, who had arrived from Oldham Athletic. The two of us worked well together up front as part of the 4-2-4 system employed by Mr Bentley and we also took it in turns to drop back and draw Woods out of the defence on occasions. All things considered, the game was a lively encounter, which also saw trouble in the crowd during the first half, officials and police having to rush into the middle of a large contingent of Stockport fans to quieten things down.

Team-mates during my time at Elm Park were never going to be big household names, although Peter Silvester went on to play at a higher level with Norwich City. There was a good team spirit, however, with the likes of Roger Smee, who went on to become club chairman, Colin Meldrum, Mike Dixon, Ernie Yard, Dick Spiers, Dave Bacuzzi, John Chapman and Dennis Allen, and who could ever forget John Collins and John Docherty? Those two were absolute nightmares. They lived in London and travelled down together each day. They could talk the hind legs off a donkey and, when meeting up at the café, they would absolutely slaughter each other about who had spoken the most on their journey. We nicknamed them 'Chirpy and Chippy' and they did not shut up, even through training. John Docherty eventually became manager at Brentford. I bet his team talks went on for hours!

As a group, we worked hard and enjoyed life as much as possible. After every home game, we would either go across the road to the Spreadeagle pub on the corner or to Ernie Yard's lodgings, where his landlord and landlady would provide an open house for all the team and throw parties for us.

At 21 years of age, I was still quite wet behind the ears, so Dennis Allen took me under his wing and helped to point me in the right direction. Dennis was one of those people who knew where to get anything or if he didn't know himself then he knew a man who did. Every Friday before a home match, we would go out to this country pub and meet up with the village butcher, who Dennis knew, and in return for match tickets and a couple of quid, we would both come away with a box containing enough meat for the whole week. This proved very handy to take home to Christine as by now we were parents to our first child, a son, Mark, and living in a club house near Prospect Park.

Assistant manager Jimmy Wheeler was a great help to me as well. Reading born, he knew just about everything about the club and the town and, having scored 147 goals in 406 league games for the club between 1958 and 1964, he also knew a bit about finding the back of the net. Unfortunately, he broke his leg at Barnsley in September 1964, which effectively ended his league career, but he continued to play and coach the reserves, captaining the side that won the Football Combination in 1966 and he later became first-team assistant manager before eventually being appointed manager of Bradford City in June 1968.

After our success against Stockport on the opening day, we went on to win six of our first seven games and I was averaging a goal a game as we challenged at the top of the league table. Our only defeat came in a bad-tempered game at Shrewsbury in early September, but the following week I scored a goal to help knock First Division West Bromwich Albion out of the League Cup. Unfortunately, we also picked up a few injuries in the early weeks of the season and, in addition to myself, our experienced right-back Dave Bacuzzi and highly promising 18-year-old forward Peter Silvester each spent time on the sidelines.

By Christmas, we had dropped down to mid-table and, although I had seven league goals to my name, I was sometimes pushed back into a deeper midfield position by Mr Bentley. In the FA Cup, we had beaten our local neighbours Aldershot in the first round but needed a replay in early January to see off Athenian League side Dagenham, a club I knew very well. My affinity with them was not enough to stop me from scoring the winning goal. Our success meant a third-round tie away to First Division champions-elect Manchester City and when we returned home from Maine Road, we were cock-a-hoop after holding them to a goalless draw. The replay did not go so well, however, as City hammered us 7-0 at Elm Park.

We finished the Third Division season in a decent fifth position, six points behind title winners Oxford United, but missed out on any chance of promotion – remember, there were no play-offs in those days. Personally, I was a little disappointed with my final tally of just 12 goals, ten of which came in the league from my 30 appearances and the other two in the cup competitions, but all things considered I suppose I had a reasonable first season. That was about as good as it got for me at Reading, though, and by the end of the following season we had a new manager and I felt my days at the club were probably numbered.

After scoring my first goal of the 1968/69 campaign in a 7-0 win against Hartlepool at Elm Park in September, I followed up with two more in a 2-2 draw at Walsall but I found opportunities to score much harder to come by after that. Performances and results became very patchy, and as the team languished in mid-table, hopes of promotion soon disappeared.

Once again, after safely reaching the third round of the FA Cup, we faced tough First Division opposition. This time we went down 4-0 to Newcastle United in front of a crowd of more than 41,000 at St James' Park. In the league, meanwhile, results also continued to disappoint and Mr Bentley was eventually sacked in the February, with club coach and former right-winger Ray Henderson taking over as caretaker manager. I had a lot of time for Ray, both as a player and as a coach, and we developed a good friendship, but the manager's job eventually went to Jack Mansell.

Mr Mansell was 41 years old and had played as a full-back for Brighton, Cardiff and Portsmouth before embarking on a coaching career at Dutch side Blauw Wit in Amsterdam in 1961. The following year, he moved to Sheffield Wednesday, then returned to the Netherlands with Tel-Star two years later. He was then in charge at Rotherham between 1965 and 1967 but came to Elm Park after a short spell in the United States, where he was manager of Boston Beacons. He was appointed on 1 April 1969, a very appropriate date as it turned out!

Mr Mansell had a reputation for producing sides which tried to play with First Division style in the lower divisions, but he certainly did not prove to be a good motivator. His first act as manager at Reading was to order the removal of a television and radio from the dressing room. Then he changed our training venue from the dog track to the local rugby ground, where even when the grass was cut short for us it was still six inches high and we had to improvise by using the rugby posts as goals, making it very difficult for the goalkeeper to make any sort of saves. No wonder so many of our shots were going over the bar on matchdays! The training was very hard and physical but not very good technically. Mr Mansell instilled a tough form of discipline, but it would have been nice to see a ball occasionally.

Our season tailed off in the end, as we lost each of our last four league games to finish 14th. I had hardly set the world alight, scoring just nine goals, and began to wonder what the future might hold for me.

Mr Mansell brought in a number of fresh faces for the 1969/70 season, including quite a few players who had played for him previously at Rotherham. I got on with really well with Bobby Williams and Les Chappell. In fact, Les went on to work for me when I was at Southampton and now lives in Torquay. Bob was living in Bristol when he moved to Reading and because we were such good mates, he moved in to live with Christine and me. We still keep in touch to this day. Former East London schoolboy Tom Jenkins was another new addition in July, the 21-year-old winger joining the club for £500 from Southern League Margate, having also had spells at Leyton Orient and West Ham.

Mr Mansell encouraged the club's promotions executive John Doe to adopt the American 'sock-it-to-'em' tactic to try and attract bigger gates. Eleven pretty girls were supplied by a local modelling agency, kitted out in team shirts, white plastic mini-skirts, white boots and white hats. As well as selling match programmes inside and outside the ground, the girls would sit at the front during matches and yell approval when we were successful on the pitch – which was not all that often, unfortunately, but it brought the club some publicity at the time. I'm not sure what people would make of it now, though!

The early months of the 1969/70 season were still hard going as Mr Mansell chopped and changed the team. By November, Reading occupied 17th place in the league table and had been knocked out of the FA Cup by non-league Brentwood Town. Bacuzzi and Silvester were amongst the players who left Elm Park for pastures new during the season, together with long-serving left-back Colin Meldrum and wingers Tom Jenkins and George Harris. Jenkins made the club a tidy profit after making a big impression during his short stay, with Southampton manager Ted Bates paying £60,000 to take him into the First Division.

To be fair, the reshaped team did put in a reasonable push for promotion in the end and eventually finished eighth. But, long before then, I had had enough of Mr Mansell and as he had selected me in the starting XI for a league game just once, I guess he was not too disappointed when I left in February 1970. I still believe today that, even at such a young age, I knew more about football then than he did.

I think that, without knowing it, Mr Mansell did me a great favour, as I went on to further my career and to better things, whereas Reading were relegated at the end of the following season and he was dismissed not long afterwards, never to manage a club in this country again.

One standout memory of my time at Reading is not directly related to football. My wife and I had decided we wanted a dog, possibly a Bassett hound. Ahead of an away game at Shrewsbury, the team were staying at a hotel in Church Stretton and the owners had an Afghan hound. Well, it was love at first sight! I asked where they had bought the dog and was told the breeder lived just down the road. I could not wait and got permission from Mr Bentley, who was manager at the time, to go and buy a puppy, and to bring him back on the team coach after the game. So far, so good!

Duly purchased, the puppy came on the coach to that afternoon's game but unfortunately the excitement and disturbance proved a little too much for him and he relieved himself during our journey to Gay Meadow. Understandably, the manager had a quiet word and suggested it might be better if I made alternative arrangements to get Sam, my name for the dog, back to Reading after the game.

Fortunately, Roger Ware, a reporter who was covering the game for the local newspaper, came to the rescue and offered Sam and myself a lift home in his car after the game. Imagine my wife's surprise when I walked in with this Afghan puppy. I had mentioned the word hound and she had expected a Bassett!

I soon found out that Sam certainly had a mind of his own. On our walks to the local park, once off his lead he would race away and disappear out of sight. It sometimes took more than an hour to get him back, but he was a beautiful dog with a natural cream coat and black ears, and he was a great companion.

Back to football and my spell at Elm Park, I made 77 first-team appearances in all competitions, scoring 21 goals and on my birthday in 2019, a supporter sent me a copy of a Reading programme which included on the cover a picture of me scoring that first goal. Happy days – mostly!

In the words of Bobby Williams

'My friendship with John began when I first met him at Reading FC in 1969. I had just transferred there after a brief, unhappy spell at Bristol Rovers and Reading were then under the new managership of Jack Mansell, my former boss at Rotherham United.

'John offered me a bed to stay at his house (unbeknown to his family). I stayed until my family relocated and he moved on to Bournemouth to continue his career. He was a talented player, strong with good ball skills and a good sportsman. I was not surprised that he later moved into coaching, managership, scouting and match analysis.

'Our friendship continued over the years as we met up at various matches. I was then scouting for Reading and John was doing the stats on the game. We also met up with other mutual friends for family events and occasions. John had an easy-going nature and was always approachable. It was an honour and a privilege to have been able to call him a friend and colleague.'

Bobby Williams served four Football League clubs, making over 320 appearances as an inside-left. He featured in 65 league games for Reading between 1969 and 1971, scoring 21 goals. His playing career was effectively ended when he suffered serious injuries in a car crash in September 1972, after which he rejoined Reading as youth-team manager.

In the words of Roger Ware

'Back in the 1960s, I was sports editor at the *Reading Chronicle*, which sold around 50,000 copies per week, a figure which I would proudly claim included almost all of the 10,000 or so regular followers Reading FC had at that time (the *Chronicle* now sells around 5,000 per week, but that's another story!)

'So, I always kept an ear to the ground for club gossip, especially around the summer when they were looking to make new signings. The pre-season of 1967/68 was no exception and one of the "little birds" who used to feed me titbits of "inside information" suggested we were about to sign a striker from Tottenham.

'That was certainly an attention-grabber. In those days, Reading had the late, great Roy Bentley as manager and the budget he was allocated by a board not noted for its generosity did not usually run to signings from the old First Division – especially a striker.

'Maybe a midfielder here and there from Aldershot or Leyton Orient, a defender perhaps from Oxford United or Bristol Rovers or a striker from Grimsby, maybe Watford. But a frontman from Spurs? Definitely time for a newshound to get digging for more info!

'It was unlikely to be either Alan Gilzean or Jimmy Greaves, the sensational duo leading the Spurs attack at the time, but quite possibly a promising youngster waiting in vain for a chance to get a first-team game with those two superstars immovably ahead of him in the chain.

'Gilzean and Greavsie – the "G-Men" – were unusual in not being the 6ft 3in tall strapping hulks typical of many strikers in those days, but perhaps Reading's mystery target fitted that bill? After all, it was also typical of the existing strikeforce at Elm Park at the time.

'However, the inside info about our incoming "Hot Spur" suggested he was not necessarily in the "bustling giant" mould. Certainly a bustler with an eye for goal, but only around 5ft 10in tall. I found out that the mystery man had a pedigree. He had played for England Schoolboys and was knocking in goals for fun in Spurs' reserves. Also, the absolute endorsement that he was probably a decent player; the legendary Tottenham manager Bill Nicholson did not sign anyone, even at junior level, unless he was convinced they had genuine ability and could have a good career in the game.

'Eventually, my snippets of info from those "little birds" were pieced together and enabled the *Reading Chronicle* to proudly break the story that the mystery man was John Albert Sainty,

21, keen as mustard and not too proud to drop down to a Third Division side in order to make his name in football.

'Make his name, John did, scoring a couple of goals on his debut and going on to net 20 in 71 games for Reading before falling out of favour when Jack Mansell took over as manager and introduced a style that did not suit John's particular skills.

'The Saint' as Reading fans knew him, was popular on and off the field from day one at Elm Park, with his friendly personality and cheeky-chappy Cockney style. He never rose to the heights of a First Division club again as a player but left behind many good memories at Reading before he moved on to Bournemouth, Mansfield and latterly Aldershot.

'Along the way, he learned the trade to such an extent that one of the shrewdest managers at the time, Bournemouth's John Bond, would take John with him as assistant manager on his journey around the top end of the game to Norwich, Manchester City and Burnley.

'So, while he never achieved top-level status as a player, John did eventually make it back to the First Division. No doubt he loved every moment of that, but I'm sure some of his happiest memories were making his league debut in the blue and white of Reading (for aficionados, firstly blue and white hoops, later Sky Blue before reverting to hoops).

'The days are long gone when local paper journalists can travel with their team, but I was lucky enough to do that. It was an experience which was not only fun for someone like me – a lifelong Reading fan anyway – but gave me the opportunity to really get to know the players. We were all good mates in those days and, valuing my friendships – and my life! – I sometimes held back slightly on harsh criticism of players I might be sitting alongside on the bus the next week. Luckily, I seldom had reason, even if I had wanted, to criticise John.

'When he moved up north, I lost track of John for a time, but after he returned south to spend his retirement in the New Forest, we renewed our friendship when my wife and I eventually moved from Reading to the Bournemouth area. Unfortunately, circumstances prevented us from getting together too often, but I'm proud to have known John as a friend and proud also to help Lindsay and Neil in their efforts to produce this amazing book!

'R.I.P. John – "The Saint"'

Following his work at the *Reading Chronicle*, **Roger Ware** continued to enjoy a prestigious career as a sportswriter with the *Daily Mirror* and the *Sunday Mirror*. He also spent five years in the international sponsorship department at Rothmans as well as seven years heading the TV production team for the *ESPN SportsCenter International* sports news show. He is currently head of commercial operations at Southern League club Bashley FC.

In the words of Reading FC club historian David Downs

'John arrived at Elm Park as manager Roy Bentley's record signing at a fee of £12,000 and immediately endeared himself to fans when he scored twice on his debut against Stockport and went on to total seven goals in his first five appearances. His goal against West Bromwich Albion in the League Cup contributed to Reading's first defeat of a Division One club for almost 40 years.

'John's second season was less successful for the club, but he continued at centre-forward under new manager Jack Mansell and remained popular with the supporters for his all-action style of play. For the 1969/70 campaign, Mansell changed the team's formation to 4-2-4, with John partnering Dennis Allen in midfield, but the season began only moderately and John soon found himself dropped. He only made three more appearances for the Biscuitmen, each as a substitute, before he moved to Bournemouth.

'John's time at Reading had been eventful but he is remembered with great affection by those of us who were lucky enough to get to know him. He went on to have a long and distinguished career in the game, of course, and served some high-profile clubs. I last met him after he had retired from football when I was working in the press box at the Madejski Stadium, commentating for Hospital Radio Reading. By coincidence, he was working as a hospital porter and providing match summaries for south coast radio stations.'

4

A FRESH START BY THE SEASIDE

BRADFORD CITY and Colchester United had both expressed an interest, but when I heard that Bournemouth still wanted me, I travelled down to Dean Court and did not take long to agree terms.

Instead of the original £12,000 price placed on my head by Spurs, Reading were prepared to accept £4,000 and, having never lived outside of an inner-city environment, the thought of living by the seaside seemed like a breath of fresh air to me and a good place to bring up a family. The deal was soon done and I looked forward to a fresh start on the south coast.

Bournemouth had finished the 1968/69 season in their highest position for five years, but moments of carelessness often robbed them of points that could have been enough for them to gain promotion. In contrast, the 1969/70 campaign appeared to be hitting the skids, with a number of senior players carrying injuries and the manager forced to blood several talented youngsters.

The club was not in a strong financial position and, with the team struggling for points, they had slipped to 18th in the table and the manager was under a lot of pressure. Having been a permanent fixture in the Third Division since the club entered the Football League in 1923/24, you might think Bournemouth were overdue for promotion, but they had an injury list as long as most people's weekly shop and their overheads were getting bigger by the day. They were reported to be losing around £1,000 a week and relegation looked a much likelier exit route from the Third Division than promotion.

In January, they had sold their most valuable playing asset, 23-year-old goalkeeper Roger Jones, to Blackburn Rovers for £30,000. It was a ludicrously low fee for a player of Roger's potential, but it was the best they could get. It left them without adequate cover and they lost their next game 8-1 at Bradford City. Just before I signed, 21-year-old Ipswich goalkeeper Alec Bugg came in on a month's loan.

When I arrived at Bournemouth, Christine and Mark remained in Reading, so I moved into digs near to the town's railway station with three other lads from the football club. Our landlady, Mrs Elkins, was brilliant to us and my rooming mate at the time was a lad from Bristol called Tony Powell. Tony had been quite a good amateur boxer in his time, hence his nickname 'Knocker'.

My first appearance for Bournemouth was at Fulham and I remember playing up front with a lad I had met only a few days previously called Ted MacDougall. Ted had been an apprentice under Bill Shankly at Liverpool but never played a first-team game for the Reds. He had scored goals regularly for York City during the previous two seasons, though, and had cost Bournemouth £10,000 during the summer of 1969. Carrying on his fine scoring record, he had already grabbed 16 goals for the Cherries in his first season and went on to head home the equaliser as we scraped a 1-1 draw at Craven Cottage.

Ted hit a hat-trick in the next game, but he was fast becoming a marked man and, as opposing defenders made it more difficult for him one way or another, he couldn't find the net with the same regularity as the season drew to its close. Unfortunately, I didn't make much impact either and, after eight games without scoring, I began to lose a bit confidence and dropped out of the side for a few matches. Results were not good; in fact, we didn't win another match until the end of March.

I returned for the last game of the season at relegation rivals Gillingham and we fought out a goalless draw, which we thought might be enough to keep us up. Gillingham had one more game to play, though, away at champions Orient and they now had to win it to secure their own safety and relegate us. Guess what – they won 2-1 and we were down.

The following week, Mr Cox was sacked and Bournemouth appointed John Bond, who had been a successful player at West Ham and latterly coach at Gillingham, the club who had effectively just relegated us. I began to wonder about my future with a new manager coming in. Being fairly new at the club myself, I did not think I would necessarily be his cup of tea and this appeared to be rubber-stamped when I received a letter from Mr Cox saying he understood that Mr Bond would possibly try to offload me and how sorry he was.

Such is life in football; one man's meat is another man's poison. I was sad about the prospect of moving on, as I had really begun to love the place and got on very well with all the players. I also had a family – by now including a daughter, Joanna – to consider, so I decided to get my head down and show the new manager that I could do a job for the team. John's former West Ham and Torquay team-mate Ken Brown came in as coach and he became the buffer between the manager and the players, which seemed to work really well.

Pre-season was brilliant, back to running and playing with the ball, but it soon became clear that John had his own ideas of the type of player he wanted and that, basically, 75 per cent of the playing squad he inherited were not his cup of tea.

After Spurs, where they played a type of football that I believed to be the best, going to Reading and initially at Bournemouth, I found the training was at odds with how I had been taught to play the game. But under John Bond, I was now really enjoying the sessions and felt that I was getting something out of them.

Even if the manager did not want me, I certainly wanted to be involved in what he was preaching. His style of play was very different to the long-ball game. He wanted to play in every area of the pitch, even from his own penalty area, for the team to pass and run, and to produce the flowing style he had played himself under Ron Greenwood at West Ham.

We still did our share of pre-season runs at Bournemouth, though, and often we were dropped off either in the New Forest or at the zigzag on Bournemouth beach and told to make our way back to the football ground! But John also introduced a new concept in training called the Coverdale Course, which was innovative at the time. It was designed to encourage positive thinking, improve efficiency and to develop co-operation. It meant hard work for the players, with sessions of four hours three or four times a week and included exercises that did not appear to have much to do with football, such as writing essays and building with toy bricks. It was unusual but it certainly taught the players a lot about their own strengths and weaknesses.

Managers need players who can implement their basic ideas on how the game should be played and ally them to their own individual abilities. Lots of players were allowed to leave the club and John signed a number of players with West Ham connections during his time at Bournemouth, including Keith Miller, who had been understudy to Bobby Moore at Upton Park, Tony Scott, Bill Kitchener, Bobby Howe and Harry Redknapp. Pat Holland also came for a short period on loan.

Mel Machin and John Meredith arrived from John's previous club, Gillingham, while Micky Cave, John Benson and Tommy Mitchinson came from another of the manager's former clubs, Torquay United. The experienced former Wolves and Cardiff City goalkeeper Fred Davies was also brought in to provide some stability between the sticks.

One of John's best signings, though, came on the recommendation of Ted MacDougall. Ted had played alongside Phil Boyer at York City and the two of them had this almost telepathic understanding up front. I sensed that things were on the change again and John decided that Phil was a better frontman than me. To be honest, I thought that too! I was moved into midfield for a time after Phil arrived at Dean Court in December 1970, which suited me much better, and I became much more involved with the first-team squad as a whole.

As well as a flamboyant new manager, Bournemouth had an ambitious new chairman named Harold Walker, a solicitor by trade but also a lifelong fan and a club director for the previous three years before taking over the reins soon after I arrived. His dream was to make the Cherries 'the Newcastle of the South' and he seemed prepared to finance it, firmly believing that John Bond was the manager to help him succeed.

Everyone at the club was enrolled on the Coverdale course and away we went.

The initial task was to gain promotion from the Fourth Division at the first attempt and we started the 1970/71 season with a bang. We blew away most of the defences in our sights, with Tony Scott providing the ammunition and MacDougall scoring most of the goals. By the end of October, he had netted 16 times and then smashed six past Oxford City in an FA Cup replay to set a new club record.

I missed only one league game during the first half of the season and chipped in with a couple of goals plus another in the League Cup at Torquay. I think it would be fair to say I did my share of the workload up front before Boyer took over. He and MacDougall again proved to be a terrific partnership and didn't take very long to replicate the success they had enjoyed previously.

Ted went on to score 49 goals in league and cup games that season to set another club record as we bounced back to the Third Division in style. Boyer chipped in with 11 of his own and we lost just one of our last nine games in the run-in. For my part, I grew to enjoy the challenge in midfield and the more games I played there, the more my confidence grew. By the end of the season, I had missed only two games and felt pretty pleased with the all-round contribution I had made.

Our reward for gaining promotion was £500 in bonus money for each player, together with a short break at Cala Mesquida in Majorca for the whole group, including wives and families. The only snag was that during our brief stay on the 'Holiday Isle' we had to play a friendly game against local side Manacor. Nonetheless, there was still plenty of time to relax and enjoy the sunshine.

The following season began with a flourish and a second successive promotion looked on the cards for much of the season. I played in most of the early games and I remember John Bond handing me the No.11 shirt when our winger Tony Scott was out injured. That was the last thing I needed. Scotty was an out-and-out winger and a good one, but I was asked to play in midfield. Nobody told the supporters that, though, and whenever I moved away from the left-hand side, they cried out to me, 'Sainty, get on your wing!' but I didn't have chance to explain.

We beat big guns Aston Villa 3-0 and soon found ourselves at the top of the Third Division, but I don't think either the players or supporters realised just what an achievement that was for a side that had just got promoted. Team spirit was high, as was competition for places. In midfield, for example, there were six or seven players in the tussle for recognition and this provided plenty of incentive to play harder and prove worthy of your place.

To help us relax during the week, the club was given the use of the sauna and swimming pool facilities at the town's East Anglia Hotel outside the holiday season, although one day our leading goalscorer got into difficulties there. Ted MacDougall and a couple of the other lads were in the pool throwing a ball to each other and, as Ted couldn't swim, he was stationed in the shallow end as usual. But as Ted lunged forward into deeper waters to try and grab the ball, he missed it and instead was taken under the water. At this point, he began to panic, so I jumped in and pulled him out. When we got back to the ground that day, I told John Bond that I had saved the club about £100,000!

The MacDougall and Boyer partnership went from strength to strength, the former this time making national headlines by creating a new FA Cup goalscoring record with a staggering nine goals in an 11-0 win against non-league Margate at Dean Court. Talking of records, our return fixture against Villa attracted a crowd of more than 48,000 in front of BBC *Match of the Day* cameras, a record attendance for a Third Division fixture at the time. We lost 2-1 this time, but the game will always be remembered by Bournemouth supporters for MacDougall's classic diving header goal.

It wasn't just Ted who was grabbing the headlines. John Bond had also become one of the most sought-after young managers in the country and was regularly linked with vacancies at First Division clubs. Despite the loss against Villa, we still looked poised for promotion again until we suffered a late sequence of six games without a win, including a highly charged 1-1 home draw against Brighton, who eventually nipped in to take the second promotion spot behind champions Aston Villa.

Throughout the season, we had been feted by the media as the best team in the Third Division, yet when the excitement ended and the promotion places were settled, we had just missed out. That we finished third with a record number of points for a club that failed to gain promotion was of no consolation. It was frustrating also because all the momentum that had been building up at Dean Court stalled and although we were quoted as the bookmakers' favourites for promotion the following season, things were never quite the same again.

After scoring 47 goals in all competitions during 1971/72, MacDougall departed for Manchester United the following September and, the first game after he left, I was selected to take his place against Shrewsbury Town at Dean Court. No pressure there then! Ted was always going to go at some point and we all wished him the best, of course. As I was wearing his

No.8 shirt, our goalkeeper Fred Davies made sure I followed him out on to the pitch as Ted had always done! As a team, we just had to get on with it, otherwise we would have just been making excuses.

We won the game 2-0 and I received praise from John Bond for my performance, but one of the Shrewsbury players obviously made an even bigger impression upon him, as he went straight out and signed him! His name was Alan Groves. Alan had tons of ability and his pace and skills were phenomenal. He was such an exciting player to watch, though you never quite knew what to expect from him. He scored twice on his debut for Bournemouth at Rotherham, but I also remember one game in which Alan tormented the opposition (I can't remember which team it was), dribbling the ball into the corner and then sitting on it and inviting them to come and get it! It wasn't something I would condone but it was an occasion that's difficult to forget. My first-team opportunity was soon thwarted once more when John signed Brian Clark from Cardiff City in a £70,000 deal and it was back to the reserves for me. In just his second game, Brian played alongside Boyer and Groves at Rotherham and scored four goals himself in a game we eventually won 7-2. Not a bad start and Brian went on to find the back of the net on 14 further occasions that season before joining Millwall the following summer.

I must admit to having felt more than a little disappointed to have lost my first-team place again but the day after the win at Rotherham, my thoughts suddenly moved elsewhere. My dad was working in a hold at the East India Docks when a supporting beam fell and struck him across the back, pelvis and legs. He did not lose consciousness but was taken to Poplar Hospital before being immediately transferred to the intensive care unit at the Royal London Hospital because of chest complications.

Thankfully, Dad slowly recovered from the initial injuries and was eventually transferred to Manor House Hospital for rehabilitation, where he remained for the next month. It was a catastrophic time for all the family and both Mum and Dad's health suffered considerably as a result. He was not able to return to work for almost a year and then was only able to do light duties, which meant sweeping and tidying, and making tea and, with no regular hours, it must have been a bitter pill to swallow, although I didn't realise at the time just how difficult it must have been for him. We were just relieved that he had survived.

I was sent out on loan to Mansfield towards the end of November 1972 but was called back to Bournemouth the following month as so many of the players had gone down with a bug and numbers were down to the bare minimum. I was really pleased, as it meant I would be home for Christmas.

Keith Miller and I, along with our wives, took it upon ourselves to organise a Christmas party for all the players' children, plus a New Year party for staff. Both proved a great success and I remember our coach, Ken Brown, saying that his children had such a good time that if a party took place the following year, they were not to be invited! Ken wondered what did go on at that party. I have to say my memory of it all is fairly sketchy, but I was just pleased that everyone enjoyed themselves.

I had a really happy time at Bournemouth. Christine and the children enjoyed living in Winton and there was a great set of players at Dean Court. Keith was my room-mate on away trips and became one of my best friends. We were allowed one glass of wine with our meal but on our away trips we would take it in turns to sneak in a bottle of wine plus a late-night snack, hot dogs usually, which we cooked in the kettle in our room! The wine helped us to get a good night's sleep and it didn't seem to affect our game the next day. However, it would certainly be frowned on today.

When we were playing at home, the team always went to the East Anglia Hotel in Poole Road for our pre-match meal. We used to eat together at noon for a 3pm kick-off and our normal meal consisted of steak and, although there were no chips, it was, with rice pudding to follow, not ideal for playing a football match a few hours later. Nutrition was not high on the list of requirements at that time. However, after a while, steak was banned and the menu became either boiled chicken, eggs on toast or cereal.

Keith and I decided, as we had a lot of time on our hands, to go into business along with our wives. We knew friends in the women's clothing trade in London, I am not quite sure how, but we rented a small shop in Southbourne and started a boutique we named Clover. Sadly, we dived in with no real idea what we were doing and were way out of our depth. Fortunately, we got out before burning our fingers too badly. Truly, we were no entrepreneurs.

The social life at Bournemouth was very good. John Bond loved spending time with the players and arranged several memorable trips to the races. He and a few of us went out on the town on occasions and also to see his favourite American singer Jack Jones at the Bournemouth Winter Gardens. Another favourite spot in town was Winston's, which was a big house in Westbourne that had been turned into a night club. At the end of each season there was an overseas tour, but one I sadly missed out on was to Australia and Hawaii in 1973 as, by that time, I had to stay behind to fulfil my youth-team coaching role.

In January of that year, the Bournemouth team coach was involved in a nasty accident whilst returning from a game at Scunthorpe. Several players suffered cuts and bruises, and coach Ken Brown ended up in hospital with a broken thigh. Trevor Hartley stepped up during Ken's period of convalescence and John asked if I would like to become youth-team coach, as I was not always called into the first team and often played in the reserves.

It was a great shame for Ken, who was very much the link between the players and the manager, and there was no doubt that he was hugely missed whilst he recovered. Nonetheless, I was not about to turn down any opportunity offered. Although it may have seemed that I was back to square one, like at Spurs, I loved it, both the coaching and the playing. It felt like exactly what I was born to do and I believed I had some ability for the first and was not bad at the latter.

Things were going along fine. I had a specific job and was involved at a club with a manager whose way of playing the game I believed in, and the nucleus of the youngsters were progressing. There were some excellent young players in a good group of lads which included Ian Cunningham, Howard Goddard and Mark Nightingale, who all went on to become first-team players, and all the lads were a pleasure to work with.

We had some notable successes, particularly in the Southern Junior Floodlit Cup. After beating Coventry City in the quarter-finals, we spent two days at the FA coaching headquarters at Bisham Abbey to prepare for the semi-final against Ipswich Town. Unfortunately, we subsequently lost that game but, at the end of the season, 15 players travelled to the Netherlands for a short tour and took part in the Groningen Youth Tournament.

Two other players I must single out were the two Kevins – Bond and Reeves. Kevin Bond was a gangly youngster whose size outgrew his strength and maybe had his dad not been manager of the football club, he may not have had the opportunity to become a professional. On the other hand, Kevin Reeves had buckets of potential right from I first saw him as a schoolboy.

On one occasion I had forgotten that Kevin Bond was an apprentice professional whereas Kevin Reeves was a schoolboy and in one youth game I played Reeves and made Bond substitute. It was soon pointed out to me in no uncertain terms that, regardless of ability, you did not play a schoolboy ahead of an apprentice – another lesson learned. Both lads went on to do well as time went on and, of course, were with us later at Norwich.

Despite Bournemouth being amongst the bookies' pre-season favourites, we missed out on promotion to the Second Division again in 1972/73, to the frustration of everyone concerned. Ken returned to his duties during the summer, although we made a poor start to the following season as well and John rung the changes. I was reinstated to the team and scored in a 3-0 win against Aldershot in September.

There was a lot going on at the club around this time, but I was determined to try and hold on to my place in the side and, with Groves falling out of favour and requesting a transfer, I returned in midfield wearing the No.9 shirt, before moving forward and reverting to the role I occupied as a youngster at Spurs.

John used 19 different players in our first four league games and took a lot of criticism from supporters, but eventually we went on an unbeaten run that lasted a dozen games and we moved quickly up towards the top of the table. In the League Cup, we took Second Division Sheffield Wednesday to a second replay before going down 2-1 in extra time. I was particularly pleased to score from the penalty spot at Hillsborough and again in the third game, which took place at Villa Park. We played 330 minutes football across three matches, which finally ended in disappointment and we felt we had been robbed as, to a man, our performances really deserved a win. Everyone had stepped up to the plate on a particularly soggy and strength-sapping pitch.

I felt some earlier performances I had shown in the reserve side were paying off, but I was blown away by the praise given to me in John's newspaper column the following Saturday, where he described my performance as 'a revelation' and added that he 'was certain that, had I had a couple of yards more pace, I had the footballing ability and knowledge of the game to have got to the very top'. Those words will always stay with me.

I knew I could run all day, but only at a very steady pace, so John's comments were very fair and the team's kit man could probably have beaten me over 100 yards!

This was, I think, the most enjoyable and productive period of my playing time at Bournemouth. The last week of October was particularly good. Another penalty at Watford came on the back of a midweek hat-trick at Aldershot, taking my season's tally to eight league and cup goals and establishing me as the club's leading goalscorer and one of the top marksmen in the Third Division.

It was probably my finest hour in a Bournemouth shirt that evening at a damp Recreation Ground against Aldershot.

Virtually half of the crowd of around 5,000 had travelled up from Bournemouth, but it looked as if it would be a disappointing night when, with only 12 minutes left, bottom-of-the-table Aldershot were 1-0 up.

That's when I stepped in. One goal came after a corner, one was a header and the third was when their goalkeeper, Tony Godfrey, rolled the ball to me because he didn't realise I was there! I always remember when I came off that John Bond didn't even shake my hand! Aldershot wouldn't give me the match ball. It was the only hat-trick I ever scored at senior level and if they had given that ball to me, I would still have it today, but they didn't, so I haven't. My tenth goal came against Cambridge United in early December but, by then I'm afraid, change was on the horizon.

As usual in football, feeling settled is not often an option and, sure enough, despite Harold Walker pleading with them to stay, John and Ken Brown left to take up new positions they were offered at Norwich City. Mr Walker, a local solicitor and truly lovely gentleman, was bitterly disappointed. He put coach Trevor Hartley in charge of the team and eventually appointed him as manager. Truly, I am not sure why, as Trevor was on a hiding to nothing. At 26 years of age, he had not long finished his own playing career – ended early through injury – and was never able to command the respect of the players, especially the senior ones. Although he had taken over first-team coaching duties for a while the previous season while Ken was recovering, he didn't impress me. I thought he was frightened of his own shadow and we certainly did not like each other very much. I remember his nickname was 'Bottle Top' because of his pale complexion and really fair blonde hair.

It became obvious to me that I would not figure in his long- or even short-term plans, but it still came as a shock when I was given a free transfer at the end of the season, despite ending it as the club's leading goalscorer with 15 in all competitions. Incredibly, I was given the news on the evening of the end-of-season supporters' party, where I was on the shortlist for being named player of the year. It could have been a real embarrassment for the club; however, I did not win and my best mate, Keith Miller, deservedly won that honour instead.

Realistically, I couldn't have stayed any longer under Trevor Hartley anyway. He was a player I played with, a coach who I worked with, but when he took charge we just didn't see eye to eye. He didn't like me as a player and made that quite obvious. These things happen in football, they happen in all walks of life, but when you love the game you just keep going and don't let things like that upset you.

I wasn't a wonderful player but the Bournemouth team at its peak was the best team I ever played in. I was the bread-and-butter type of player in that team, not one of the stars, but every team needs its workhorses. I wore every outfield number except two, three and five for Bournemouth. My favourite number was always eight but after Ted made that number his own, there was no chance of me getting that again whilst he was there and he was always going to be a difficult act to follow.

So, time to move on, where would fate take me now?

In the words of Ken Brown

'When I came to Bournemouth as coach with John Bond in 1970, John Sainty was already on the playing staff at Dean Court and, with him also being a Londoner, we were never short of a word or two! He, of course, hailed from Poplar, whereas I came from Forest Gate. My background was with West Ham, whilst he was a Tottenham boy, but we didn't let that stop us from soon becoming friends! Bondy and I quickly became aware of Saint's adaptability as a player and, although he did not always feature in the first team, he was a tremendous asset to have in the dressing room. We knew that he was always around when we needed him and, whether playing up front or in midfield, Saint could always be relied upon to give nothing less than 100 per cent.

'In addition to his playing ability, Bondy noticed that Saint was someone who could communicate well with others and able to pass on clear instructions during a game. As a result, he began to involve him in coaching the youngsters and it soon became clear that he was very comfortable in this role, too.

'So, as well as being a player, John began to develop a second string to his bow and it was one that we would benefit from again later in his career.'

Ken Brown made close on 400 Football League appearances for West Ham during a playing career that also saw him make one full international appearance for England. After ending his playing career, the former defender teamed up with John Bond as coach and assistant manager at AFC Bournemouth and Norwich City. Brown eventually took over from Bond as manager at Carrow Road in 1980 and five years later brought the club success in the League Cup Final at Wembley. He subsequently managed at Plymouth Argyle and worked as a scout for England managers Terry Venables, Glenn Hoddle and Kevin Keegan.

In the words of Keith Miller

'John was a great team-mate and friend. We became room-mates on away trips with Bournemouth and soon found we had a lot in common. Both of us liked a laugh and a joke, and John was always ready with a gentle anecdote on life! Mind you, he could be quite cutting at times.

'He was football mad and a great person to have in the dressing room. I would describe him as "a wonderful club man". John probably underachieved a little as a player and I certainly think he underrated his own ability. He was a very reliable and adaptable player who seemed to have 360-degree vision and was always happy to play in whatever position the team required.

'Bondy certainly took to him and soon spotted John's ability to coach. He was good at conveying the right information to young players in a personable sort of way and those players respected him for that.

'John liked dealing with all sorts of people inside and outside of football, and he and I even entered the fashion business together. Neither of us really knew what we were doing, and it didn't last long but it was fun at the time!

'Although our careers took us in different directions, we always remained in touch, and I miss the company of this lovely, lovely man.'

After being understudy to Bobby Moore at West Ham for five years, **Keith Miller** captained the Bournemouth side that won promotion from the Fourth Division under John Bond in 1971 and went on to make a total of 383 Football League appearances for the Cherries during his ten-year stay at Dean Court. He later managed in non-league football at Dorchester Town, Fareham Town and Poole Town.

In the words of Ted MacDougall

'John typified the spirit of the club during the early 70s. Nobody worked harder from the start to make himself a good player.

When he switched from striker to a midfield role, it gave him fresh confidence in his ability.

'He was always good technically, though, very knowledgeable about the game and didn't hesitate to give you his opinion. He was certainly no shrinking violet!

'When John scored his hat-trick at Aldershot, I was living in London, having a bad time of it playing for West Ham but still following Bournemouth! The game was played in midweek, so I was able to go along and watch. We won 3-1. I was thrilled for John and went down to the dressing room afterwards to congratulate the team. When I walked in, John jumped up and shouted out, "The King is dead, long live the King!" It was not exactly what I wanted to hear at the time, but it was typical of John's dry sense of humour and nobody could have deserved that hat-trick more than he did!'

Ace marksman **Ted MacDougall** was the Cherries leading goalscorer in three successive seasons between 1969/70 and 1971/72 after joining the club from York City for £10,000. The former Liverpool apprentice moved to Manchester United for a club record fee of just over £200,000 in September 1972 before teaming up again with manager John Bond at Norwich. Whilst at Carrow Road, he became the First Division's leading scorer in 1975/76 and won seven full international caps for Scotland.

In the words of Kevin Reeves

'I was born in Burley in the New Forest and Bournemouth were my local team. My first recollection of Saint was as a fan. I used to stand on the South End at Dean Court as a young teenager and remember the promotion in the 1970/71 season. Looking back, we had similarities, both in size and build and in the position we played in the team. Like myself, he wasn't a

No.9 but played off the main striker. He had a great touch and a strong lower body, which enabled him to hold off defenders, and was an intelligent player.'

Striker **Kevin Reeves** started his career as an apprentice with AFC Bournemouth before making his Football league debut for them in the 1974/75 season. In 1977, John Bond took him to Norwich City for £50,000 where he played 133 games and scored 42 goals before joining Manchester City in March 1980 for £1.25m. Reeves scored 39 goals from 158 appearances in all competitions whilst at Maine Road, including a penalty in City's defeat in the 1981 FA Cup Final. He also made two appearances for England at full international level but was forced to retire from the professional game due to injury at the age of just 26.

In the words of Kevin Bond

'My first recollections of Saint came when he was a player at Bournemouth. They had a good side then and were very entertaining to watch. My father liked him, not only as a player because he could play in a number of attacking positions, but also as a coach. With his knowledge of the game and interest in the coaching side, it became clear he would make a good coach when his playing days were over.

'John was the first coach I ever had as a youngster at Bournemouth. There were lots of doubts as to whether I would make the grade in my early years. John would have shared them too, but worked really hard with me and all of the youngsters every day in order to make sure that we gave ourselves the best chance. He was a good coach and it was no surprise that he went on to work alongside my father with the first team at Bournemouth and later at Norwich and Manchester City.'

Kevin Bond began his playing career as an apprentice at AFC Bournemouth where his father, John Bond, was manager. He later followed his father to Norwich City, where he made 142 Football League appearances before teaming up with him again at Manchester City in 1981. After 110 appearances for City, he moved to Southampton, where he spent four years, playing 140 games. After his playing career ended, he took to coaching and worked alongside manager Harry Redknapp at Portsmouth, Southampton, Tottenham and Queens Park Rangers. He also managed AFC Bournemouth for two years between 2006 and 2008.

In the words of Steve Gritt

'My recollections of John Sainty are mainly from the team that was assembled by the manager at the time, John Bond. I would be taken to Bournemouth games in that 1970/71 season by my dad and remember it being an attacking and free-scoring team which included the likes of Ted MacDougall, Phil Boyer, Tony Scott and John Sainty. With John being a forward player, it was always going to be difficult to displace the MacDougall-Boyer partnership, so John became an energetic attacking midfielder, chipping in with some important goals during that terrific promotion-winning season. It is fair to say that John played his part in the Bournemouth team of the early 1970s that, in my opinion, will always be remembered as one of the best under the stewardship of John Bond.'

Steve Gritt went on to become an apprentice and later full-time professional with AFC Bournemouth between 1974 and 1977. Most of his playing career was then spent at Charlton Athletic, for whom he made 347 Football League appearances. He became joint manager in 1991 and helped to lay the foundations for that club's future success under Alan Curbishley. Steve also managed at Brighton and returned to AFC Bournemouth as chief scout between 2011 and 2012.

In the words of Glenn Stride

'I vividly remember watching from the stands at Dean Court as Saint played for the reserves with all of his youth-team looking on. Bournemouth were winning the game and he had already scored twice when they were awarded a free kick on the edge of the penalty area. Saint was standing over the ball while the opposing goalkeeper was standing at his near post marshalling his wall.

'Saint then had a word with the referee, took the free kick and curled the ball into the unguarded corner of the net to complete his hat-trick. He was delighted, more so than usual because he had all of his young charges watching him do it!

'One Saturday morning, we were travelling to London to play Spurs in a youth league game. We travelled by minibus and Saint was at the wheel. We arrived without any problems but promptly lost the match. After the game, we set off for home and it seemed to be taking a long time to get out of London. I was sitting in the front of the minibus and was just about to ask Saint if we were lost when we pulled up outside a house. He looked across to me and said, "Just dropping some duty free cigarettes off to my old man." Brilliant! An extra hour on our journey home, but who cared?

'Another memory of our time together occurred when we went to Holland to play in a youth tournament against other European clubs. We got to the semi-final – or final? – and the game ended in a draw, so it went to a penalty shoot-out. We lost that and the trialist who missed his penalty was devastated. I was first back to the dressing room and Saint was sitting inside. He hadn't watched the penalties at all and told me: "They don't mean anything, we drew that match."

'Over the next decade, I saw the England team get eliminated from several competitions by losing penalty shoot-outs. Whenever it happened, I wondered if the England manager was telling his players what Saint told me?'

Glenn Stride was an apprentice professional and member of the AFC Bournemouth youth and reserve teams between 1972 and 1975.

In the words of Chris Giles

'I recall playing for Bournemouth's youth-team against Newport County at Parley Sports Ground during the 1973/74 season. John was the club's youth coach at that time.

'Newport had a lively and talented left-sided midfield player and he was running the game. I was playing right-back and I believe we were losing by the odd goal at half-time. John was quite animated at the break as he gave his team talk and he gave me specific instructions to "nobble" the Newport playmaker by way of a tackle, to "slow him down" as it were.

'I did enjoy a tackle and was competitive but was surprised to receive such instructions from John. I did as I was told and put in a fair but firm tackle early in the second half and the player had to be substituted.

'Unfortunately, it was not the player John had identified and a few choice words were shared at the end of the match!'

Chris Giles was an apprentice professional and member of the AFC Bournemouth youth and reserve teams between 1973 and 1976.

5

MY FOOTBALLING DISASTER!

AT THE age of 26, I was at a crossroads. My playing career seemed to be going nowhere and it would be fair to say that offers were not flooding in.

I loved being involved in coaching but really wanted to continue playing for a few more years. Surely there had to be a manager out there looking for a battering centre-forward or a plodding midfield player, albeit, in all fairness, one with good vision, who could pass the ball and had an eye for goal? With a wife and two children to look after, the only manager who seemed to be showing an interest in me was the bank manager, who was not going to be too pleased if I did not get an offer quickly.

Eventually, the offers did come and I had a choice to make. An offer arrived from a team in South Africa and another from the USA. Closer to home, Torquay and Aldershot were both interested. Torquay seemed miles away and I was doubtful whether I could make a life outside the UK. Aldershot offered me a signing-on fee of £1,000, which at the time I was extremely grateful for, so the decision was made. In hindsight, I wish had taken the opportunity to go overseas.

I would politely describe my time at Aldershot as a footballing disaster. If I *thought* I knew more about football than my last manager at Bournemouth, Trevor Hartley, I *definitely* knew more about it than my new manager at Aldershot, Tom McAnearney! I soon discovered that he had signed me mainly because I had scored my one and only league hat-trick against them the previous season. I remember being disappointed after the game that Aldershot would not allow me to keep the match ball as it was the only one they had! I should have seen the writing on the wall then.

My league debut for the Shots came on the opening day of the 1974/75 season and it became something of a double-edged sword. I came on as substitute against Hereford United in a game we eventually lost 2-0. As if that wasn't bad enough, someone, somewhere had not finalised the paperwork regarding my registration and the club was fined £200 and handed a one-point deduction. Come the end of the season, we only just missed relegation, ironically finishing just above Bournemouth, who went down to the Fourth Division.

Fortunately, the team spirit was tremendous, but the trouble was, most of the spirit was mostly in the pub! There was a mixture of lads, mainly at the wrong end of their careers, who bonded well together despite the manager. Some of them thought we had three managers actually – Tom, Mac and Ernie! Lenny Walker, Murray Brodie, Joe Jopling, Glen Johnson, Jack Howarth, Terry Bell, Ray Dean, Pat Morrisey, Malcolm Crosby and Richard Walden were all good lads, along with a few others whose names slip my memory but whose exploits do not!

Our daily routine was similar to that at Reading, all meeting up each morning at a local café near the ground, then training, back to the café, betting shop next door, pub and home. The manager took charge of the team on matchdays but normally left training to the coach, John Anderson. It was awful, very physical, very dreary and very boring. Every week of the season we had the same sessions, so we all knew what was coming next. Every Monday afternoon, we would gather in the dressing room while the boss held an inquest into Saturday's game. Nobody ever said much. It was the best way of keeping the meeting short and once Tom got it off his chest we could go.

The home team dressing room had a sauna in one corner and the skips, used for packing boots and kit for away matches, stood in front of the sauna. Tom would always stand in front of these skips to hold these inquests, cleverly keeping himself warm from the heat of the sauna, while we all sat on the other side of the dressing room, freezing.

One particular day, I remember Tom was a little late, so Terry Bell decided to climb inside one of the skips. Tom arrived and started his inquest. He was in a good mood because we had won on the Saturday. We were finding it hard to keep a straight face, but Tom didn't cotton on and then asked, 'Terry did you not think …' At the same time, he was looking around, as he couldn't see Terry. He then asked, 'Where is Terry?' The reply came back, 'Here, boss.' And, at the same time, the skip began to move forward and Terry popped his head out of the skip. We all fell about laughing, but Tom told Terry to get out, stop messing around and got on with the team meeting. On the pitch, after winning our first two games of the season we were soon struggling and ten matches went by before we won again. We went out of both cup competitions at the first-round stage and spent most of the season anchored near the bottom of the league before eventually finishing 20th. That we avoided relegation was mostly down to three consecutive victories gained in late March and early April. We didn't win any of our last five games but somehow managed to stay just outside the bottom four.

I found myself in and out of the side during the season but managed to complete 29 appearances, playing mostly in midfield. My former Reading colleague Terry Bell was our leading scorer, albeit he only found the net on eight occasions. In previous seasons, Aldershot had relied on the prolific Jack Howarth up front, but Jack was injured for a large part of the second half of the season and his goals were badly missed.

When we stayed in a hotel overnight before an away match, the manager always allowed us one pint of beer with our meal. To most of the lads, this was not enough, so once we were settled into our rooms, we would always meet in the nearest pub simply by saying we were going for a walk, turning right and walking round the block. We could do this quite safely as Tom always had the same habit of turning left, leaving us free to get away with a couple of drinks before returning for our meal and our one permitted pint!

We certainly had a lot of fun together as a team and I remember we hired a coach at the end of the season and went for a day out at Lingfield races. It was a good day out, too, with me eating four lots of jellied eels plus drinking a few pints. We finished our trip with a stop-off in Brighton, but as we made our way back on the coach, some lads in another coach parked next to us started to give us some stick, having somehow found out we were Aldershot FC. They challenged us to a race over a mile, for which the distance was marked out to the far fence of the coach park and back, and it was suggested their best runner should compete against ours.

I found myself selected, not because I was the fastest but because I was one of the few still able to stand up straight! With honour at stake, off we went. This other lad started off really quickly and I hoped he would blow up before long, but no such luck. However, halfway down the coach park I noticed a small stream lay in our path and this lad started to hesitate as he approached it. I shouted at him, suggesting we had gone far enough and perhaps we should turn round and race back. As he turned, he was suddenly hit by both cramp and a stitch, and could only manage to walk back, whereas I jogged home to win by a distance – unlike any of the horses I had backed that afternoon! At least honour was restored to Aldershot FC!

During the summer of 1975, I spent a week away in Majorca with the family, where I met up again with Ken Brown, who was also on his family break. We soon got talking about football, of course, and Ken explained how big a job John Bond and himself had taken on at Norwich. He mentioned that they were keen to build up a good youth policy, so I asked Ken to seriously consider me if they were able to get the scheme off the ground.

The summer break always went by so quickly and this one was no different in that respect and I was soon back home, trying hard to get some of the weight off that I always seemed to pile on in the close season. My physical efforts over the years were beginning to take their toll by now, a result of either battering the opposition or being battered by the opposition! The wear and tear on my left knee, in particular, was beginning to cause problems. I would wake up each morning only to find that it took longer to get out of bed and get going and I was having to walk up and down the stairs to get any ease of movement. Training was becoming difficult and I knew I was on borrowed time.

Once pre-season was over, I again felt things were not looking particularly good for me. I had not been included in many pre-season games and things came to ahead when I was called into Mr McAnearney's office one morning. Apparently, someone had reported seeing Jack Howarth and myself drinking at Epsom races 48 hours before a game. The fact I had not been selected to play in that game didn't seem to matter and I was told to look for another club. Jack, however, did play in that game, but I guess Tom was not going to leave himself without his best player and leading goalscorer.

My time at Aldershot was up, so remembering my holiday conversation with Ken Brown, I called him and he said that if I could obtain my release, there was a job waiting for me at Norwich. And this is where the sting in the tail came from Aldershot. I could get my release straight away, but they wanted my £500 signing-on fee back in return. My dad came to the rescue. Nothing ever seemed to be a problem to him – except me! The money was paid, although Aldershot retained my playing registration, so my playing career was over aged 28, but I was off to rejoin John and Ken, to set up a youth policy at Carrow Road. My playing days were behind me and my next step was to be a good coach, the best I could be. Would I? Or did I really want to eventually become a manager? Time would tell.

Years later, I would go to Aldershot quite regularly whilst working for the Press Association and soon discovered I am best remembered there either for scoring a hat-trick against them or for costing them a point by playing when not properly registered!

In the words of Neil Warnock

'I was a young player going away from home for the first time down south and John took me under his wing and really helped me to settle.

'He had such a calming influence about him but also such determination to be the best at all times.

'I took some of John's traits around with me throughout my career as a player and a manager and will always be grateful for his help.'

Neil Warnock played for eight Football League clubs and was at Aldershot between 1975 and 1976. After his playing career finished, he managed 16 different clubs from the Premier League to non-league. He holds the record for the most promotions in English football, with eight, and the most games as a professional manager, with over 1,600.

In the words of Malcolm Crosby

'When John joined Aldershot in 1974, I was a 20-year-old cheeky Geordie. John was 27 and a London lad that soon put me in my place!

'We got on well off the field but sometimes on the pitch it was different. The problem was that I had no energy and no brain, whereas John was technically good and also had a good football brain.

'Lots of players will say that John was a good player and I find it difficult to see why he only played 29 games for Aldershot.

'We always had a good laugh at training as he had such quick wit, so it was important not to get involved with the Saint as he was so sharp with his answer!

'In later years, during the 1990s, I would bump into John at games and we would sit and chat throughout enjoying talking about players and ex-managers. I think we would both forget why we had gone to the game!

'John was a top person and a very dry, sharp and funny man.'

Malcolm Crosby made 294 Football League appearances for Aldershot between 1972 and 1981. As caretaker manager he took Sunderland to the FA Cup Final in 1992 where they lost to Liverpool. He is currently chief scout at Exeter City.

In the words of Graham Brookland

'I got to know John during my time as head of media at Aldershot Town FC. John was a representative of the Press Association where he used to provide minute-by-minute updates on the matches at Aldershot home games during their time in the Football League between 2008 and 2013.

'It was a long time before I realised that John had had such an extensive footballing career, including representing Aldershot as a player in the 1970s. We had some fascinating conversations about his time in football and I thoroughly enjoyed meeting him on matchdays at the Recreation Ground.

'It is testament of the man that he did not discuss his achievements in football in the press box. These were notably superb, not just as a player, but as a coach and manager, too. Ironically, the press box always consisted of experts in their field, journalists writing their scripts on the matches without ever realising that the biggest expert of all was sitting in the back row of the press box, quietly and diligently going about his business.'

Graham Brookland has over 30 years' experience within the football industry, notably with Aldershot Town FC and the Army Football Association. His roles with the Shots have included company secretary and head of media.

6

IN TUNE WITH THE CANARIES

SO, WE were off to Norwich and the First Division!

With City struggling near the bottom of the table, chairman Arthur (later Sir Arthur) South had fallen out with manager Ron Saunders after a three-year tenure and, as I mentioned earlier, appointed John Bond as the club's new manager in December 1973.

Ken Brown came with him as assistant manager and, inevitably, some of Bournemouth's best players would follow them to Carrow Road. Cherries favourites John Benson, Fred Davies and Mel Machin went immediately, soon to be followed by Phil Boyer. It caused a lot of unpleasantness between the two clubs that would last for several years to come, during which time several more players would follow the same path.

Bondy's big target, though, was to re-sign striker Ted MacDougall, who had by then joined West Ham United after a brief, unhappy spell at Manchester United. Things weren't going well for Ted at Upton Park either, so naturally he jumped at the chance to reunite with his old boss at Norwich. Many Norwich supporters were not in favour of the move, however, as fans' favourite Graham Paddon went to West Ham in exchange as part of the deal.

John's first home match at Carrow Road was against Liverpool in December. Conditions were wintry to say the least. Welcome to East Anglia! But a crowd of over 20,000 braved the elements to see how the new management team and players would perform and the fans left fairly satisfied after a 1-1 draw. A humorous moment came when the referee, Derek Nippard, ironically from Bournemouth, had a snowball thrown at him by Liverpool's Alan Waddle for refusing to award a free kick.

A Boxing Day loss to arch East Anglian rivals Ipswich Town made things a little uncomfortable, though, despite Ted grabbing a trademark MacDougall goal, seizing a half-chance before anyone else could react.

Three defeats in four games were followed by a further five losses, which had supporters asking questions, but gradually Ted became more settled and, with the rebuilding of the team, more positive signs were on the way. The masterstroke came with the subsequent signing of Boyer to re-establish his partnership with Ted while John continued to rebuild the nucleus of his side. Unfortunately, relegation could not be avoided at the end of that season, but City bounced straight back into the First Division the following year.

Tony Powell was another former Cherries player who had found his way to Carrow Road and another important signing had been midfielder Peter Morris from Ipswich. But in March 1975, John had pulled off something of a coup when he signed the great Martin Peters from Tottenham for £50,000. City finished third behind champions Manchester United and runners-up Aston Villa and John had also guided them to the League Cup Final, which they lost 1–0 to Aston Villa at Wembley.

The family and I soon settled in our new home in the small market town of Wymondham, just to the south-west of the city. It was quite unlike anywhere we had lived before, but easily accessible to the A11 and the main route to London, so getting to see my mum and dad was quite straightforward. It proved to be a good spot to escape from the day-to-day hubbub of football life, despite being only a short walk from the town.

At the time, the Norwich training ground was at Trowse, a small village to the south-east of the city. It no longer exists today and, in its place, a small housing development has been built on the site. In addition to John and Ken, the management set-up when I arrived also included Terry Medwin, who took charge of the reserve team. John wanted to bring youngsters through the ranks along similar lines to the highly regarded set-up he had known at West Ham, but there was no real youth policy when he arrived and youngsters playing local league football were not usually good enough to progress into the professional game.

My task was to find a team of good, skilful players who would become so successful that the side would be broken up. That may sound a little strange, but the idea was that if they did really well for me and got their chance in the reserves, then I would know I had done a good job. To gain a pool of young players, I contacted the local education department and asked for the name of the best school and best PE teacher to contact and was put in touch with Graham Wren at the Hewitt School, which had an excellent sporting reputation, and with Graham's help the process of setting up the youth development squad began.

The set-up took shape really quickly, particularly considering the geography of the club and the fact that our nearest neighbours, Ipswich Town, also had a youth policy. Every day, training was full-on and, just as I had done at Spurs, the first item on the agenda was for the lads to check all boots and kit were ready and waiting for the senior players before they could begin their workout.

John Bond liked his team to be full of flair and skill; that was his mantra and mine was no different. The players had to be themselves, but doing well on the field meant playing skilfully in readiness for them to move up into the reserves and eventually the first team, who set the style of play for the whole club.

He wanted his youth players to play against similar young players in the South-East Counties League – the likes of Chelsea, Arsenal and West Ham – but as most clubs in the league were a travelling distance of a good two and a half hours away, the authorities turned down John's initial application. After he had done a lot of lobbying with other managers, we put in another application, adding a proviso that during our first season we would play all our matches away from home. In addition, for the second season, opposing clubs would be given the option of travelling to us or not. This time we were successful and, thankfully, before the third season it was deemed agreeable that clubs would have to play us both home and away, which meant a few less early morning starts!

On one occasion, I remember leaving at 6.30am to go to Portsmouth, where first we played at their Barracks training ground with an 11am kick-off, then played them for a second time with a 3pm kick-off at Fratton Park. It only happened the once and I made sure it wasn't repeated! They were long days spent travelling and playing each week and it also meant the lads had very few opportunities to watch the first team.

Apprenticeship was not an easy road and it was not always for everyone, but I estimated to have watched 240 boys in trials during my first season. Sifting out the good from the not-so-good was quite a task but, helped by chief scout Basil Hayward, we felt we did a pretty good job. I also ran a keep-fit class one evening each week and reinstated my old trick of running around wearing a polythene bin liner to help lose weight. I had used this technique to try and shed a few pounds during pre-season training at Bournemouth, despite making an audible 'crinkling' sound whilst exercising! Old habits die hard!

Meanwhile, John had a very happy group of first-team players to fall back on, who desperately wanted to play for him in the First Division. We finished tenth in the club's first season back and whilst Liverpool were winning the Football League Championship, mid-table security was a very satisfactory finish for the Canaries.

At 31 years of age, Martin Peters soon corrected anyone who thought he was past his best and was behind just about everything that was created on the pitch. Meanwhile, Ted MacDougall plundered 23 goals, including two hat-tricks in the space of four games and one of City's goals in a famous 3-1 win against Liverpool at Anfield in November 1975.

As for myself, I was gaining lots of knowledge and experience, and training and coaching methods were continually evolving. Keeping players fit can be a problem because, when working with a group, certain running and exercises can only be basic. I found at all levels that some players needed specific workouts – for example, stamina, sprinting, weight-training (both light and heavy) – so they were all given an individual plan which would enable them to peak, both mentally and physically, on matchdays.

A couple of other players I knew from Bournemouth had by this time also made their way to Norwich – David Jones and Mark Nightingale. David had been my team-mate and now I was one of his coaches. As well as the youngsters, we had a good group of senior players at Carrow Road which also included Colin Suggett, Duncan Forbes, Kevin Keelan, Billy Steele and, of course, Martin Peters to name just some of the great professionals I was also privileged to work with.

John frequently enjoyed a dabble in the transfer market and there were plenty of ins and outs at Carrow Road the following summer, including Morris and club legend Dave Stringer. John Ryan came in from Luton, but the biggest exit was MacDougall, who longed to return to the south coast where he had business interests and, in October, he joined Southampton.

Fulham's 26-year-old striker Viv Busby was Ted's replacement, but things took a while to get going and, after losing at Liverpool on the opening day, City managed just one win in their next six games. Their best run of the season came over the festive period when they won three games on the trot followed by a 2-1 win in their return fixture against Liverpool at Carrow Road. Martin Peters put us ahead from the spot after a quarter of an hour and the score remained the same until Jimmy Neighbour doubled the lead in the final minute. Neighbour had arrived from Tottenham the previous October and the goal was his first for Norwich. There was still time for Phil Neal to snatch a penalty for the visitors in the last seconds.

January also saw another former Bournemouth player transferred to Norwich, with 19-year-old Kevin Reeves moving up from the south coast for £50,000. Kevin was very young when I was at Bournemouth and had since been handed his league debut by my former team-mate John Benson, who had returned to Dean Court to take over as manager in 1975. I knew Kevin was an outstanding prospect. He was not the bravest player, but he had pace and natural ability, and he certainly knew where the goal was. I soon found that he embraced any position he was asked to play in and it was a pleasure to play a further part in his development.

The low point of City's season came in February, with a 5-0 thrashing by Ipswich at Portman Road, a result that also saw our arch-rivals briefly go to the top of the table. Even more frustration was to follow when the Tractor Boys won 1-0 at Carrow Road in April to complete a league double. We finished the season in a somewhat disappointing 16th but at least we had guaranteed our place at the top table for another season. To his credit, Busby ended the campaign as our top scorer with 11 goals, his finest hour coming on New Year's Day when he hit a hat-trick in a 3-2 win against visitors Leicester City.

John's fourth season with City, 1977/78, saw us finish 13th and maintain what might be called mid-table mediocrity, but there was always something going on at Carrow Road. The previous year he had signed a right-back called John Ryan from Luton Town for £40,000. However, by his own admission, Ryan was not the fastest defender and sometimes found difficulties when faced with marking a speedy winger. So, recognising his immense stamina and prodigious workrate, Bondy moved him into midfield. It proved a masterstroke, as Ryan went on to score 15 goals and was eventually named player of the season.

We kicked off the campaign with a 3-1 win against West Ham at Upton Park. After the game, our team coach was parked next to a hall where a wedding reception was taking place and it was soon surrounded by guests, bridesmaids and even the bride herself, who posed for a photograph with Martin Peters! Unfortunately, it proved to be the only away win we would manage all season.

Boyer joined Southampton for £135,000 and our other main striker, Viv Busby, departed for Stoke in December, leaving our attack in the hands of Reeves and 24-year-old Keith Robson, a £25,000 signing from Cardiff City. We enjoyed a few highlights during the season and even managed to beat Liverpool and Ipswich at home in December, although the bragging rights returned to Suffolk the following March after we were thumped 4-0 in the return at Portman Road.

After the departures of MacDougall and then Boyer, in all honesty we were struggling to find a fitting forward partner for Reeves, who continued to impress and ended the season with 12 goals from 37 league appearances. Robson had been the most effective but, in the summer of 1978, I persuaded former Tottenham and England striker Martin Chivers to return from Switzerland and join us, only for him to be thwarted by injury after a bright start.

Our biggest win of the season turned out to be a 4-0 success against Birmingham at Carrow Road in September, with goals from Reeves, Chivers, Robson and Ryan doing the damage against a side that would eventually be relegated. This was part of a bright start we had made to the campaign, beating a newly promoted Southampton team, which included Ted MacDougall, 3-1 in Norfolk on the opening day and also winning three and drawing three of our opening eight matches.

Davie Robb, a similar style of player to Chivers, then arrived from United States club Tampa Bay Rowdies but he did not stay long. One of our younger prospects, Phil Lythgoe, had shown promise when called upon but by the end of 1978/79 season, there was a new kid on the block and his name was Justin Fashanu.

Fashanu was the son of a Nigerian barrister living in the UK and a Guyanese nurse. When his parents split up, he and his brother, John, who was 19 months his junior, had been sent to a Barnardo's children's home and then, aged six and four, respectively, placed with foster parents in the village of Shropham in Norfolk.

I was made aware of Justin when he was 13 through Graham Wren and I was impressed by his football potential whilst watching him play a match for his school, Attenborough High, against Thetford Grammar. I invited him to come along and train with the Norwich youth-team squad and soon after he signed as an associated schoolboy for City and eventually as an apprentice. He was a difficult child to deal with in a number of ways and certainly had some raw edges, but when he got out on the pitch, he was a real handful there, too, and gave us something different.

John Fashanu started the same journey towards a career in the game a year later, purely because big brother Justin was doing so well. Along with Ronnie Brooks, who did a lot of the pastoral work with the youngsters, I talked regularly to the Fashanu boys' foster parents, Alf and Betty Jackson, and took a genuine interest in the two boys, as well as coaching them.

Both lads were tall, strong and athletic and Justin also excelled at boxing as a youth. He was streets ahead of all the other youngsters for pace and strength, but although a prolific goalscorer, he had a long way to go to catch up on the skills required to become a good all-round performer. He practised when and where to make his darting runs, developed a more delicate touch and gained better close control of the ball.

Justin turned professional in December 1978 and made his Football League debut against West Bromwich Albion the following month. He did well enough to feature in another 14 games that season, scoring five goals.

We became the country's 'draw specialists' in 1978/79, with no fewer than 23 of our 42 league games ending all square. Between October and March, we even managed a hugely frustrating run of 14 draws in 18 league games. Mind you, it proved enough to secure a fifth consecutive campaign of top-flight football and we finished the season in 16th place. Between December and February, we even managed to draw seven consecutive league games, which I believe was a record for the club at the time. Reigning European champions Liverpool proved far too strong for us as they reclaimed the First Division title from Nottingham Forest, winning 4-1 when they visited Carrow Road in October and 6-0 at Anfield in February.

There was a worse club record we also achieved, though, as we failed to win any of our 21 away matches. It must have been a torrid time for the travelling supporters, as this meant that we had not won away since the opening day of the 1977/78 season. Thankfully, the awful run ended with a 4-2 win at Everton on the opening day of the 1979/80 campaign.

It was good to see my former Bournemouth team-mate Tony Powell named as our player of the season after he completed a third consecutive season without missing a game. Tony was originally a forward who had first been converted to a left-sided midfielder, before John moved him to left-back and finally centre-back. He arrived at Carrow Road as part of a swap deal for Trevor Howard after City had been relegated to the second tier in 1974 and had quickly established himself as a consistent presence with a very firm and determined style. Tony stayed for seven years before moving to America, where he played for San Jose Earthquakes before leading a rather colourful life in Hollywood after his playing days were over.

Martin Peters once again led the side by example during his third season as skipper and the World Cup winner was given a guard of honour ahead of a 1-0 home loss to Everton in November. A few weeks earlier he had celebrated his 35th birthday and had been made an MBE for his services to football.

After our bright start to the previous season, we made an even better opening to the 1979/80 campaign and this time we were able to maintain it for a much longer period until injuries finally took their toll.

We won eight and drew six of our first 20 matches and by the end of January we were fourth in the First Division table behind Liverpool, Manchester United and Arsenal. A League Cup charge had also seen us knock United and West Bromwich Albion out before Liverpool intervened with a 3-1 win at Carrow Road in the fifth round. Justin Fashanu made a storming start with a brace during a 4-2 win at Everton on the opening day. He also scored in wins over Tottenham, Nottingham Forest, Bolton and Southampton, as well as another brace in a 2-1 home win over Crystal Palace as results picked up after a disappointing February and March.

Our injury problems had seen centre-backs Tony Powell and Phil Hoadley out of action and reached new levels when Kevin Keelan broke a finger during a 5-3 home defeat to Liverpool in February. That began a run of ten games without a win, with back-up goalkeeper Roger Hansbury stepping in for Keelan. It gave opportunities for more of my youth-team players to come through the ranks and into the first-team squad, including Greg Downs and Peter Mendham. Greg was originally a centre-forward, but he switched to left-back early in his career and went on to play 169 league games for Norwich, while Peter was a tenacious midfielder who enjoyed ten years at Carrow Road.

Another change in circumstances was afoot and came about literally by accident. Ken Brown was the victim, sustaining an injury which meant he was not going to be fit to carry out his duties at Carrow Road for some considerable time, so John Bond promoted me to first-team coach over Terry Medwin, which did not go down too well with Terry. A few days later, John and I went to watch a game in London where we bumped into John's old manager at West Ham, Ron Greenwood. I was introduced as the new first-team coach and he informed Ron that he had promoted me from youth-team coach. Mr Greenwood shook my hand and congratulated me but added that it is always better to keep your best coaches with the youth team, so as to bring the youngsters on with knowledge and experience.

From youth-team to first-team coach is a big leap. With the youth team, you are primarily a teacher, looking after your pupils and nurturing their development. Crossing the big divide meant working with experienced First Division players, who all have ability and their own ideas – some good, some bad. With 15 to 20 professionals in the squad, it is down to the coach to produce a capable team which the manager can then turn into a successful one.

By now, I had realised that amongst the different characters and personalities you encounter at every football club, you are usually also fortunate enough to meet and work with players that ooze quality and I was now about to work with one of the best; Martin Peters, aka 'The Ghost'. What could I tell him though? Much of what I knew, I had learned from him in the first place.

Martin is someone I will never forget. He was ahead of his time and could see things that were about to happen before they did. One of my first and lasting impressions of him was his ability to read the game so well and the more options a player has, with or without the ball, determines how good he is. Most players' options are either to pass or to run and more often than not they choose the wrong option. Martin was so clever, he could pass to a minimum of three different players, not only start a move but also visualise the next step, hardly ever lose possession of the ball, make runs into space and receive the ball, and make space for others. Although many professional players have some of these abilities, Martin possessed them all, plus endless others, and, despite not being the best tackler, he had the ability to read where passes were intended to go and intercept them. He could go through games without over-exerting himself and I think that's another reason why he was able to play so effectively for so long.

Even with Martin's experience on board, we began to sink towards the battle for survival, though, until goals from Fashanu and defender David Jones earned a galvanising 2-1 home win over Arsenal and, after winning four of our final seven games, we ended up in 12th place.

Around this time came the controversial sale of our star player Kevin Reeves, who became one of the first British players to be sold for £1m when he joined Manchester City in March. Malcolm Allison's City, who were below Norwich in the table and only just clear of relegation trouble, decided to splash out on the 22-year-old, who had earned his first England cap in November after nine goals in his first 20 games of the season with us.

John Bond was naturally disappointed to be losing Reeves and made his feelings clear, although he understood the financial implications. The supporters were not quite so forgiving, however, with the famous banner of 'No Reeves, No Fans, No Hope' appearing as Kevin scored during his final appearance for the Canaries, his 42nd goal in 133 league and cup games, in a 2-2 draw with Brighton.

Clive Woods was soon brought in from Ipswich to provide experience on the wing and allow Keith Robson to partner Fashanu in attack. There was no doubt the Canaries had a rising star on their hands as Justin scored 12 goals in 41 games in all competitions. There was one Fashanu goal in particular which is remembered among the most famous in the Canaries' history, his spin and volley from just outside the area during the 5-3 defeat to Liverpool in February. It went on to be named goal of the season by the BBC and has since become iconic.

Another player who excelled during the season was Kevin Bond. In 1974, at 16 years of age, Kevin had moved from Bournemouth up to Norwich to join his father and initially had to overcome the inevitable accusations of favouritism. Since then, I had seen him grow into a first-class footballer after making his league debut at Leicester in 1976. He had been ever-present in 1978/79 and then contributed an impressive 11 goals from right-back in 48 appearances during the 1979/80 season. Kevin was awarded the Barry Butlin Memorial Trophy as City's player of the year and when Martin Peters called time on his distinguished Canaries career during the summer, Kevin became captain.

The experienced former Everton, Manchester City and England striker Joe Royle joined us in the summer of 1980 and probably the high point of the next season was a 5-1 win against Stoke on the opening day in which Fashanu hit a hat-trick. By now, John Bond had managed to keep Norwich in the top flight, despite the financial constraints he was under, for five seasons. He was, of course, still ambitious to try and further his career and more than a little frustrated by the lack of resources at Carrow Road, so when Manchester City chairman Peter Swales offered him the manager's job at Maine Road in October 1980, John accepted. He then invited John Benson and myself to join him, while Ken Brown took over as manager at Norwich.

I really enjoyed my time at Norwich. In the later years, each Friday after training had finished and we had a home game the following day, we would head to the tennis court for a doubles match. I loved my tennis and had even thought of trying for a career in the game when I was a teenager. Anyway, it was always Bondy and Ken against me and Mel Machin, who had by then taken over from Terry Medwin as reserve-team coach. These matches were always fiercely competitive and Mel and I were always determined to win, which we often did. Each time we were successful, it prompted the same ritual, with John 'sacking' both Mel and I only to welcome us back the next morning!

On away trips, I always roomed with Bondy and I remember one Friday evening we were in Manchester, where we were due to play United the following day. After our evening meal at the hotel, he went missing, which was strange, as normally we would sit down over a few beers to discuss tactics and team selection.

Nobody seemed to know where he had gone, so eventually I went to bed. When John came in at about 1am, he was hobbling and hardly able to walk.

John had a reputation for being a smart and snappy dresser and because we would be seeing his very good pal Ron Atkinson, the United manager and another with a reputation for snappy dressing, John had bought a new pair of shoes. He had decided to break them in that night by walking to the home of Manchester City chairman Peter Swales, who had invited him, unbeknown to us, to discuss the position of manager at Maine Road. Breaking in his new shoes resulted in painful blisters on both heels. He was in agony, but it had obviously been worth it!

Whatever club you go to, you meet people who become friends and, at Norwich, kit man Ronnie Brooks was the 'go-to' man. He was a great help to myself and my family when settling into the area. I also made firm friends with Frank South, son of the Norwich City chairman Sir Arthur South, and his family plus, of course, Graham Wren, who I mentioned earlier. Graham became a good friend and remains so to this day. I am, in fact godfather to one of Graham's daughters. Many a relaxing time was spent at Frank South's house, where he had a full-length bowling green in his back garden, and we always had great times with plenty of food and drink.

Norwich were relegated at the end of the 1980/81 season but promoted straight back to the First Division a year later. The fans were able to enjoy Justin Fashanu's talents on the pitch for a little longer but, after scoring 40 goals in 103 games, he made an ill-fated move to Nottingham Forest for £1m in 1981. After spells at other clubs such as Notts County and Brighton, he went on to play in America, of course, and that period of his life has been well documented. Sadly, he took his own life in 1998, having struggled with tabloid newspaper coverage after becoming the first openly gay professional footballer. His brother, John, turned professional just as Justin was transferred to Forest, but he never became a regular player at Carrow Road and his career and personality were developed further at Wimbledon, of course.

In the words of Ken Brown

'Saint did a great job with the youth set-up at Norwich. He proved to be a fine ambassador for the club in local schools and was always prepared to put himself out to give the youngsters every chance of success.

'When given the chance to work with the senior players later, Saint was able to step up accordingly and, together with John Bond, Mel Machin and myself, formed an integral part of our management team at Carrow Road. We became a close-knit group and often met up outside of football together with our families, when Saint could relax and allow his keen sense of humour to come to the fore!

'I last saw him at a reunion for AFC Bournemouth's 1970/71 promotion-winning side in 2021. I was so sorry to hear of his sudden passing.'

In the words of Kevin Bond

'Over the years, our two families got to know each other very well. There was a close connection, especially at Norwich, with my father's coaching staff. Every Thursday evening, Ken Brown, Mel Machin, John Benson, Fred Davies and Saint would all come to our house with their wives for a glass of wine and cheese and biscuits, with the inevitable long debates over football. They were great days.'

In the words of Ted MacDougall

'John was a very good coach; his thinking was ahead of his time in some ways. He was always interested in the nuances of the game and could be very informative. He would be able to assess a player quickly and spot their strengths and weaknesses. Sometimes he could be in your face but he talked to players of all ages in a way they could understand.

'Bondy saw John's potential early on and, although Saint was never one to propel himself forward, we all knew he had tremendous ability.'

In the words of Greg Downs

'I first came across John Sainty when, in 1975, he became the youth-team coach at Norwich City. I had been associated with the club since January 1974 and became an apprentice in the March of 1975.

'One of John's first tasks was to take the youth team to a tournament in Augsburg, Germany, in the summer of 1975. It was there that John's insight became apparent as he quickly realised that the home crowd would be quite biased towards the German teams. So, he went out before the first game and bought some footballs, which we, the players, gave out to the youngsters in the crowd before kick-off.

'In the second game, he found out that it was to be played on the German equivalent of Mother's Day, so this time he went out and bought roses, which we then gave to the ladies in the crowd. By the time we played in the final we had become the "housewives' choice" and were cheered loudly by the home crowd.

'It showed that John understood the pressures on players and looked for ways to alleviate it. He also played a large role in my life in that he was still the youth coach when I was offered a full professional contract. In those days I was a striker and had learned a great deal from John in my development.

'It was testament to John's coaching abilities that when John Bond left Norwich for Manchester City, he took John with him as one of his coaches. I didn't see John for many years after that, but we met again when he was coaching at Stockport and I was manager at Hereford United. We had a good chat, naturally about football. It shows how much John loved his football by the way he managed to stay in the game in many different guises. I am sorry to say that I didn't see him again after our meeting at Stockport as, when my time was up at Hereford, I returned to Norwich, where I still live.

'I would like to say a big thank you to John for all his help and advice during my apprentice days and feel very sad at his passing.'

After making his Football League debut in 1976, left-back **Greg Downs** remained at Carrow Road until moving to Coventry City in 1985. He was a member of the Sky Blues' FA Cup-winning side in 1987 and went on to serve Birmingham City and then Hereford United, where he spent two seasons as player-manager. After retiring from professional football, in 1995 Downs joined the police force.

In the words of Peter Mendham

'Whenever we were training and the lads had to see what their weight was, the coaching team would get very competitive about losing a few pounds themselves. That would be all of them – John Sainty, of course, as well as Bondy (John Bond), Ken Brown, Terry Medwin and George Lee.

'It was your John, Lindsay, who came up with the idea of using black bin liners to help them shed a bit of excess weight. They were big ones as well. He'd cut a big hole in the bottom for their heads and then two smaller ones for each of the arms.

'These bin liners were so long that, once they pulled them over their heads and arms and down their bodies, they'd go right down and even past their thighs! They'd all go off on a run, John motivating everyone as always. That was one of his great strengths as a coach; if you were down or needed a lift, John would be there for you, he'd soon pick you up again.

'Underneath the bin liners, they'd all be wearing their coaching tops, which were 100 per cent cotton and were very thick. It meant, as they all ran, the sweat poured from their bodies and would be absorbed by these tops until they were absolutely dripping wet – and I *mean* dripping. They'd be drenched.

'We (the players) found it quite funny, to be honest. Especially as they'd work so hard with these bin liner tops on to sweat off a few pounds then, that same evening, all go out for a meal together. They did all like a meal out did John, plus Bondy and Ken Brown. Very fond of good dining they were. So, they soon put on the pounds that they'd lost at training earlier that day. Of course, this meant that, come the following morning, out would come the bin bags again and off they'd all go. John loved it. I wonder if all the others were as keen on it as he was?!'

After making his first-team bow in 1978, midfielder **Peter Mendham** was a member of the Norwich City team that won the Milk Cup in 1985 and the Second Division championship the following year. He played in 267 first-team games and scored 29 goals for the Canaries before being forced to retire because of injury in 1987.

In the words of Kevin Reeves

'When I joined Norwich in 1977 as part of the exodus of players that went from Bournemouth to Norwich, I re-joined the coaching team of John Bond, Ken Brown, Mel Machin and Saint. It was a massive learning curve in my career. Saint and Mel would set up all the training sessions and John Bond would intervene to highlight what he wanted at certain times.

'Saint's sessions were always structured and well organised. John was very much an attacking coach and the fact that he had played in a similar role to me meant there was an understanding of what was known as the 'Strikers Union'. When I wanted extra finishing sessions, Saint was always willing to set them up and I remember him coming back in the afternoons during my time at City and the sessions were always varied and enjoyable.

'Saint had a really dry sense of humour but was a firm character and commanded my respect as a young lad. He wouldn't hold back sometimes but was fair and you knew where you stood with him. That said, you could also confide in him and talk to him. I believe Saint was largely responsible for Justin Fashanu coming into the club. He got into the team at a young age and I was fortunate to play up front with him for a season. We struck up a great partnership and it was one of my favourite seasons at Norwich.'

In the words of Graham Wren

'After graduating from Loughborough College, where I had written a thesis on football in schools, I took this qualification into teaching and continued to study football with a special interest in coaching. I was teaching at a large comprehensive school in Norwich when I first came across John Bond, who introduced me to a youth-team scout called John Sainty.

'During a televised interview in 1975, John Bond stirred up a hornets' nest by blaming the lack of quality in young footballers on their schoolteachers. This really upset teachers locally, so much so that they demanded a meeting with John Bond and his staff to discuss this issue. From this meeting, I was asked to liaise with the football club staff to bring young players to the club and to organise an end-of-season tournament to bring the best talent to their attention.

'The staff member who I was to work with was youth-team manager John Sainty. Lots of stories had emerged about John as a hard taskmaster who demanded the very best from his charges, but from this moment a beautiful friendship was born. This friendship grew stronger, both professionally and socially, until John's untimely death in 2023.

'Professionally, Saint encouraged me to extend my coaching qualifications and helped me become the very first youth development officer at Norwich City. Later, he helped me to move into scouting for Manchester City, Chester, Southampton, Stockport County and Fulham, where I still work today.

'Socially, our families spent vast periods of time in one another's company and he became a godparent to my oldest daughter. Our families travelled to Florida for a two-week football coaches exchange in 1978, where we studied at the very highest level at Nick Bollettieri's coaching school.

'In fact, throughout John's career, I moved with him both professionally and socially, enjoying his friendship whilst gaining experience of top-level coaching, which was put to good effect in coaching the schoolboy teams that I was involved with in Norwich. All my school teams were eventually called the Saints and played in full Southampton FC kit, supplied courtesy of Saint.

'To say that he was an influence on my life is a total understatement. John was a brilliant coach who worked at the very highest level from schoolboy and youth teams to Premier League international players over a 35-year period.'

After 34 years working in the education sector, **Graham Wren** is now senior academy scout at Fulham FC, having previously worked in a similar capacity at Liverpool. Since scouting at Southampton when John was academy director, Graham has also served at Glasgow Celtic, Portsmouth and Middlesbrough.

In the words of Mick Dennis

'I used to call in at the training ground at Trowse on most mornings and I remember John as a very helpful, friendly guy who was very much part of what would now be called the football leadership team.

'Obviously, John Bond set the tone and was clearly in charge, and Ken Brown was his right-hand man, but Saint was always involved in the discussions at Trowse about individual players, tactics and so on. Terry Medwin and Ronnie Burrows were others who were part of the coaching team, but neither of those two had the ear of Bondy as much as Saint did.

'I recall writing a piece about Justin Fashanu before he broke into the first team, which was prompted by Saint. I was struggling for something to write about in the *Pink Un* football paper and asked Saint if there was anyone in the youth-team who would make an article. I recall him saying something like, "Well, there is Fash, a kid who can't stop scoring goals." So, I interviewed Fashanu and I am certain that was the first piece anyone wrote about him.'

Mick Dennis was the football correspondent of the *Eastern Daily Press* for three seasons before heading to Fleet Street. He went on to enjoy a career of more than 40 years in newspapers, writing for *The Sun*, *Sunday Times*, *Daily Mirror*, *Daily Telegraph*, *London Evening Standard* and *Daily Express*.

7.
CITIZEN SAINTY

AS ON many occasions when a manager moves on to a new club, he prefers to take along his coaching staff, and when John Bond left Norwich and became manager of Manchester City, he offered John Benson and myself the opportunity to join him as assistant manager and head coach respectively. Bondy knew he could sometimes come across as dictatorial when carrying out his duties and I believe he felt the need for a support network.

Moving is always difficult. So far, I had lived in London, then on to Reading, Bournemouth, a short loan spell at Mansfield, then on to Aldershot and Norwich. The family had settled in well to the way of Norfolk life, but when opportunities present themselves, they must be embraced and so Manchester beckoned and, with it, a return to big city living.

Initially, Christine, Mark and Joanna moved into a hotel along with the two other Johns' families. This all sounds great at first, but it soon becomes trying and you long to move into a home of your own. Eventually, we found a house in Cheadle on the outskirts of Manchester and the kids settled into their new schools.

Our four months in the hotel had included the Christmas holidays, when the hotel closed down to give staff some time off. This meant we had the run of the place as if it was our own home. I was in charge of Christmas lunch, which I had always cooked since being a young lad and enjoyed doing so immensely. So, it was turkey and all the trimmings for 20, but there was no way I was going to do the washing up!

City were well down in the First Division table but, with hard work and determination, John Bond and all the staff turned things around, quite comfortably avoiding relegation. It is well documented that Bondy was not particularly welcomed from the outset by all directors at the club. I am sure it must have hurt, but he never made us aware of the difficulties he had. Instead, he just swallowed them and got on with the business of making a success of our tenure. He knew how to do his job and was more than capable of holding his own, although there were run-ins with some of the directors on a few occasions.

Our start was not great. We lost our first game through a last-minute penalty and fell to the bottom of the league. The players seemed, at first, unable to understand the tactics we wanted, but we soon began to instil some confidence into both the players and the supporters. The younger lads like Dave Bennett and Tommy Caton flourished and enjoyed playing each game with the simplicity and style that Bondy inherited from his time at West Ham as a player. That was his mantra and it was endorsed by all of us on the staff. The fact that he had cost a million pounds didn't seem to be a burden for Kevin Reeves to carry around anymore, with everything geared around the front two players. We began to climb the table and Bondy won the manager of the month award for both November and December 1980 as we went on a run which brought just two defeats in 15 games.

Meanwhile, he had already agreed to take part in a fly on the wall documentary filmed by Granada TV that had commenced during the reign of his predecessor, Malcolm Allison. The documentary featured not only the end of Allison's reign, but also John's interview prior to being handed the manager's position and the first meetings we had with the players. Never shy of publicity, his philosophy, man management and approach to the game quickly registered with the players and supporters, and they got to know pretty soon about the way he operated.

Training at Manchester City was no different to that at Norwich; you soon adapt and get to know what and who you are working with. John wanted a fairly simple style and pattern of play with as few complications as possible and was happy to leave coaching and fitness to the coaching staff. All the first-team squad at Manchester City were better players than I ever was. I was working with the likes of Tommy Booth, Joe Corrigan, Paul Power, Ray Ranson and Dennis Tueart, but I never doubted my ability as a coach. You just have to quickly gain the players' confidence and trust, otherwise chaos reigns.

The players never questioned my abilities from day one and I believe they had complete trust in me. My coaching philosophy was to treat everyone equally; there were no individuals, just a complete team working as one. I always believed I could get the best out of individuals and, although working with the first team was completely different to working with youth players, I was confident in my ability to keep them fit and interested whilst training.

John used to let me plan the sessions on a daily basis, though we would liaise and discuss anything in particular he wanted me to work on with the team or with an individual. I always knew he had complete faith in my ability and, working together with Benno and physio Roy Bailey, everything seemed to work really well. We all worked with the same philosophy. I used to sometimes room with Roy on away trips and our working partnership was always harmonious.

The players' attitude is always the key to success, though. They must want to play for the club and not just for the financial rewards. Our squad was boosted by the arrival of experienced players like Bobby McDonald, Tommy Hutchison and Gerry Gow. They gave the team more stability and each one became a firm favourite with the supporters. Gerry cost £175,000 from Bristol City and proved to be a big presence in midfield, despite having dodgy knees which regularly needed cortisone injections to get him through games. Bobby and Tommy both joined us from Coventry City for fees of £270,000 and £47,000, respectively. Bobby was particularly good at anticipating a pass and was a great reader of the game, saving him from tackling anyone or from heading the ball in defence! Tommy, even at 34, was an exciting former Scottish international winger who was also able to play infield and always capable of producing something extraordinary with the ball.

We managed to filter them into our system in both training and playing and change what they had been used to doing with their previous clubs. Another player who was extremely well known to us also made his way to Maine Road, and that was Phil Boyer. Having played under John at Bournemouth and Norwich, Phil teamed up with us again following a £270,000 move from Southampton. Buying in experienced players like these to play alongside younger team members boosted both the morale and confidence of the team and proved invaluable. It was a shame that Phil's career at Manchester City was blighted by injury and that he was only able to make a handful of appearances.

Training sessions usually ended with a regular routine. You could guarantee the time was 11.15am, when Bondy's car would arrive at the training ground car park. The two Johns would jump out wearing their training kit, which meant it was time for us to end our session and get ready to pick two teams for a small-sided game. The boss would always pick which team he fancied playing with and the game would commence with me as referee. Whatever decision I gave, he would hardly ever agree with it!

On home matchdays, I would often first go to the training ground at around 11am with our physio Roy Bailey, as our goalkeeper Joe Corrigan's preferred pre-match routine was to work out for an hour before a game whenever possible. Then it was off to Maine Road where I would meet up with the other two Johns and we would settle down to lunch in John Bond's office and discuss tactics for the upcoming game.

We always tried to keep the players calm and relaxed before a game. Eddie Large was a regular visitor to the City dressing room before kick-off, telling jokes. In addition, Graham Carr was our scout and he sometimes brought along his son Alan, who was taking his first steps towards becoming a comedian.

The chairman, Peter Swales, was a firm backer for Bond and initially supported everything he tried to achieve. By mid-January, City had risen to 11th place in the First Division and the team were really enjoying themselves, playing for one another in a simple and thoroughly entertaining fashion. John had instilled great confidence in the players; they were all playing for each other and believing in their abilities. Working with them all each day was a real pleasure and they all responded extremely well.

It was a great time for us all at the club and only around four months in, not only were we progressing in the league, but we were also bowling along nicely in the League Cup and eventually reached the last four. It was a great time for us all at the club and it happened very quickly.

The first leg of the semi-final against Liverpool drew a crowd of 48,000 to Maine Road but turned out to be a night of great misfortune as, in the opening minutes, a goal by Kevin Reeves was disallowed by referee Alf Grey for what he described as 'illegal jumping'. Our players, management and coaching staff were beyond furious, not to mention the supporters because the goal was perfectly good and should have been allowed. Reeves made a legitimate jump for a cross with Liverpool full-back Alan Kennedy without climbing on anyone's shoulders, Ray Clemence came out but never got anywhere near the ball and they all tumbled over before Reeves got up and headed the ball into the net. Kevin was adamant that there had been no foul but, ultimately, we had to travel to Anfield a goal down and feeling very aggrieved.

Sadly, that disallowed goal cost us dearly as, although we drew 1-1 in the second leg, Liverpool won the tie 2-1 on aggregate and went on to win the cup, beating West Ham in a replay at Villa Park.

We turned our attention to the FA Cup, which produced some very interesting ties, starting with Crystal Palace in the third round. Palace were struggling at the bottom of the First Division but were by then managed by former City manager Malcolm Allison and the pairing of the two clubs attracted a lot of interest and publicity. The game itself was tightly contested to begin with but thankfully in the second half Kevin Reeves scored his first-ever FA Cup goal from the penalty spot and further goals from Boyer, Power and Reeves again brought us a 4-0 victory.

Spirits were high and the irony continued in the next round when we drew Norwich City, but there is never a time for sentiment in football and the lads produced a brilliant game. Former Canaries player Reeves scored the first of the goals which saw us run out 6-0 winners. There were also goals apiece for Gow, Power, McDonald, Steve Mackenzie and Dave Bennett, although we lost Phil Boyer to a serious knee injury in the 15th minute. Ironically, the injury came after an innocent tackle from John Bond's son, Kevin. At the end of the match, John tried to clamber from the directors' box into the players' tunnel to console his son but lost his footing and instead crashed to the ground, landing on his back, and was lucky not to do himself more damage.

Fourth Division Peterborough United were our opponents in the fifth round and, with John Bond suffering from flu and John Benson also indisposed, I was left in charge of the team. Fortunately for me, Tommy Booth, who had been recalled in place of the younger Tommy Caton, proved the perfect choice and scored the only goal as we emerged as 1-0 winners. The players responded completely to my instructions and I could tell they were really up for it, which makes a coach's job a lot easier. I remember Kevin Reeves later described this game as 'one of the toughest games on our route to the final'.

I was left in charge of the team on two further occasions at City when neither of the other two Johns, Bond or Benson, were in attendance. On the second occasion, Bondy had organised a trip with an agent to travel to Sweden to play a friendly against

Stockholm FC. Sadly, I don't remember if we won, but I do remember the players did not want to be there and neither did I! The third occasion was another of John's end-of-season organised trips and the itinerary read something like this:

Fly from Manchester to Heathrow and from there to Spain; three-hour coach ride to our destination, arriving at 23.00.

Play friendly game next day against local team to celebrate local festivities, then three-hour journey back to airport to return to Heathrow.

On arrival back to Heathrow, fly straight out to Canada to play Vancouver Whitecaps in a friendly on an all-weather pitch; three days in Vancouver, then return to Manchester.

Not an enjoyable trip for anyone. No wonder the other two Johns opted out! Anyway, back to the FA Cup and we were now just two games away from Wembley and faced a quarter-final against Everton at Goodison Park. This tie proved a little more difficult and we took some time to get going. With Tommy Booth suspended, there was less experience in the side, although we did bring back City favourite Dennis Tueart in place of young Dave Bennett. But our naivety led to a penalty award for Everton which helped them to a 2 – 2 draw and a replay four days later on a muddy pitch at Maine Road. We made no mistakes at the second time of asking, though. Two goals in quick succession were created by Hutchison and scored by McDonald, and another goal from Power made us 3-1 winners.

So, there we were at the semi-final stage for a game at Villa Park against Ipswich Town, who were chasing the treble of league, FA Cup and UEFA Cup. At the end of normal time, the match remained goalless but then our captain, Paul Power, very much a local lad with a burning ambition to lead the team out in a Wembley final, fittingly became the hero, scoring the only goal ten minutes into extra time to take us there for a very auspicious occasion, the Centenary FA Cup Final.

In the days and weeks leading up to the final, there was a terrific buzz around the blue half of Manchester, with every City fan in a euphoric state. In the week leading up to the final, we stayed at the Selsdon Park Hotel, travelling down on the Tuesday, then relaxing and training down there. Unfortunately, Phil Boyer suffered the heartbreak of missing out on the game due to injury. So, always keen to keep a settled side, Bondy was determined to keep the XI who beat Ipswich, despite lobbying from the media to include Tueart. Dennis knew this but he never let his head go down or sulked in training. There was no place for the experienced Tommy Booth either, although I know these were difficult decisions for John to make, as both had played their part in helping the club reach Wembley.

How ironic for me that Spurs should be our opponents. Much was made that the final was being played in the Chinese year of the cockerel and that Spurs had won major competitions in five previous years ending with a one. There was also 'Ossie's Dream', the song Spurs recorded with fans Chas and Dave about Argentinian international Ossie Ardiles and his dream to win the FA Cup at Wembley, which reached No.5 in the charts. In fact, everything seemed to indicate that Lady Luck would be firmly on Spurs' side.

From the Manchester perspective, local broadcasters Radio Piccadilly set up in the hotel itself and carried daily updates and interviews, and there were various functions held through the week. When the big day came on Saturday, 9 May 1981, our journey to the stadium seemed to take ages, but the players appeared relaxed as they were interviewed for TV on board the coach. The memorable part came when we travelled along Wembley Way, passing fans waving flags and giving us encouragement. Well, the City fans were, anyway! Not all of them had tickets, unfortunately, and a couple of friends of mine were offered £500 for theirs; not that they would have sold them, although they did say it was tempting.

Tottenham had a very good side and were particularly strong in midfield where, in addition to Ardiles, they had the very talented Glenn Hoddle. But we felt we had just the man to upset their rhythm and detailed Gerry Gow to sit on Ardiles throughout. Whilst the two managers led their respective teams out on to the pitch, we coaching staff had to slope off round the sandy greyhound track to our seats on the halfway line. The team began well; we soon got on top and were dominating the game when we took the lead in an unexpected fashion in the 30th minute. Tommy Hutchison looked to flick on a cross from full-back Ray Ranson, but he caught it wrong and instead it rocketed into the net.

It was all looking good until ten minutes from time when Ardiles escaped Gow, who tracked back and fouled him on the edge of our penalty area. Hoddle, of course, was a free-kick specialist, so goalkeeper Joe Corrigan carefully lined up the defensive wall, but Hoddle's shot towards the near post took a deflection off Hutchison's shoulder and flew into the far corner of net. Tommy had now scored for both teams!

The game went into extra time, with both sides trying, without success, to summon up a winning goal and the outcome was only the second drawn final in FA Cup history. In the dressing room, the boys were feeling down, having done enough to win the game and perhaps sensing a great opportunity had been lost, having dominated the large majority of the 120 minutes.

The club had arranged a reception at the Royal Garden Hotel in Kensington that evening before we travelled back to Manchester the next day. My children would often remind me in later years that on cup final day, all the wives, including my wife, Chris, and Janet, John Bond's wife, were interviewed on television by comedian Jimmy Tarbuck. Media-friendly as ever, Bondy himself also appeared as a contestant on a special edition of the popular TV gameshow *Punchlines*. The TV coverage caused great excitement for them and, in those days, the build-up for the cup final would start on the Friday evening and continue throughout the following day, with players, supporters and celebrity fans filling the hours leading up to kick-off. That probably was more of a highlight than the actual match!

We returned to the Royal Garden Hotel ahead of the replay on the Thursday night. When the game got underway, another Argentine, Ricky Villa picked up a loose ball to put Spurs ahead after only seven minutes, but a brilliant volley from Steve MacKenzie and a cooly taken Kevin Reeves penalty saw us 2-1 in front early in the second half. With 20 minutes remaining, however, Garth Crooks levelled for Spurs and soon afterwards Villa began an amazing run through our defence to score a goal which has since been played back on television more than any other in a cup final. It was a great goal but one that we should have prevented.

Sadly, it was not to be our night and we were inconsolable after the final whistle, rueing not having taken our opportunity to win on the Saturday. The players put so much into that first game that they found it difficult to match it in the

Mum and Dad, Albert and Lilias, on their wedding day. (Author's collection)

Here I am at a tender age with 'Little Nan' at home in Poplar. (Author's collection).

With the Barking Boys side. I'm third from the left in the back row next to Ben Embery, I think! If I'm correct, then that's Ben's twin brother Bill, second from the right in the front row!
(Author's collection)

England Schoolboys v Wales, Vetch Field, Swansea, 24 March 1961.
I'm standing fifth from the left with Howard Kendall on my right and goalkeeper Alan Ogley to my left. In front of us are Glyn Pardoe (third from right) and John Sissons (second from right), whilst reserve Peter Storey is seated on the floor, far right.
(Author's collection)

JOHN WILL BE PLAYING IN GERMANY

BARKING schoolboy soccer hero, John Sainty, is a cert for the English Schools F.A. tour of Germany.

As Barking's third-ever schoolboy international, I was proud to wear my England Schools cap. Author's collection)

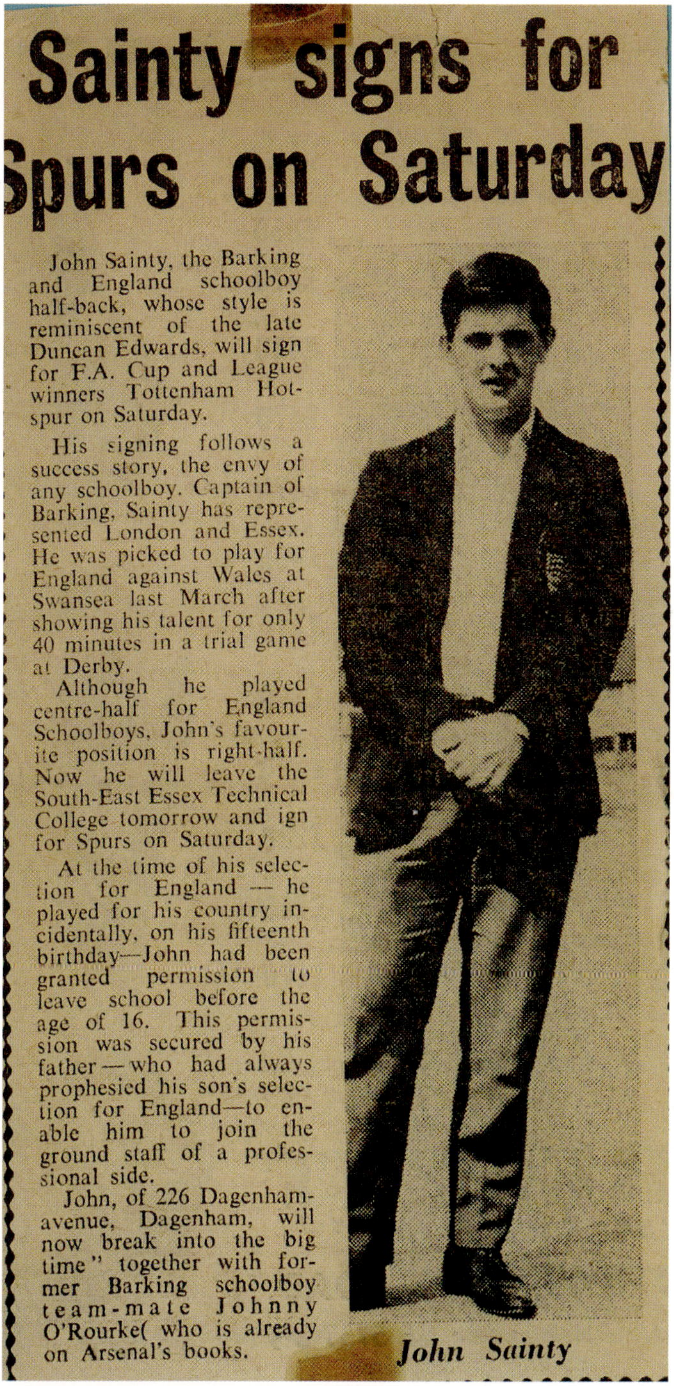

Sainty signs for Spurs on Saturday

John Sainty, the Barking and England schoolboy half-back, whose style is reminiscent of the late Duncan Edwards, will sign for F.A. Cup and League winners Tottenham Hotspur on Saturday.

His signing follows a success story, the envy of any schoolboy. Captain of Barking, Sainty has represented London and Essex. He was picked to play for England against Wales at Swansea last March after showing his talent for only 40 minutes in a trial game at Derby.

Although he played centre-half for England Schoolboys, John's favourite position is right-half. Now he will leave the South-East Essex Technical College tomorrow and ign for Spurs on Saturday.

At the time of his selection for England — he played for his country incidentally, on his fifteenth birthday—John had been granted permission to leave school before the age of 16. This permission was secured by his father — who had always prophesied his son's selection for England—to enable him to join the ground staff of a professional side.

John, of 226 Dagenham-avenue, Dagenham, will now break into the big time" together with former Barking schoolboy team-mate Johnny O'Rourke(who is already on Arsenal's books.

John Sainty

My footballing journey begins and I'm off to White Hart Lane. Author's collection)

With so many of my heroes during Tottenham Hotspur's photo call at Cheshunt ahead of the 1963/64 season. The trophy at the front is the European Cup-Winners' Cup which Spurs had won at the end of the previous campaign. In an off-guard moment, Dave Mackay and Danny Blanchflower appear to be enjoying a chat, whilst Ron Henry can't bear to look! I'm the proud youngster in the centre of the back row next to England international centre-forward Bobby Smith. (Author's collection)

Alongside another England international, centre-half Maurice Norman. (Getty)

Manager Bill Nicholson (far right) is on hand at London's Liverpool Street Station to greet the Spurs youth team upon our successful return from tournaments in Rotterdam and The Hague in 1965. I'm squatting down on the left next to my mate Keith Weller, taking in every word the Boss is saying. I had scored our winning goal in the final against Arsenal, and I seem to have brought quite a few other souvenirs back with me too! (Atkins Photos)

What a lovely couple! I was best man at Keith Weller's wedding, and our roles were reversed a few months later when I married Christine. (Author's collection)

Dancing with Little Nan at my 21st Birthday party. (Author's collection)

A proud grandad with baby Mark – that's my dad with mum, my first wife Christine and I at a family function in the late 60s. (Author's collection)

Scoring my second goal on my Football League debut for Reading against Stockport.
(Author's collection)

Back in the 1970s players would take on odd jobs during the summer months to earn an extra bob or two. At Bournemouth in June 1971, David Jones and I had the task of painting part of the main stand at Dean Court. Good job we were not afraid of heights!
(Bournemouth Evening Echo/Author's collection)

Comedians Mike and Bernie Winters were enjoying a summer season in Bournemouth during 1971 when they dropped in to see us at training. Bernie doesn't seem to be enjoying his spell in goal though as, from left to right, Fred Davies, Keith Miller, Tony Powell, Bernie's brother Mike, John Benson, Tony Scott and I let fly some quick-fire shots!
(Bournemouth Evening Echo/Author's collection)

Best left until the summer! Cherries coach Ken Brown (second left) seems to be feeling the chill, as he, Keith Miller, John Benson and I join the Bournemouth Spartans for their first winter dip of 1971/72.
(Author's collection)

Keith Miller and I knew nothing about the fashion business so naturally we decided to open a boutique in Southbourne Grove, Bournemouth. The lady in the middle was the brains of the business! (Bournemouth Evening Echo/Author's collection)

After my hat-trick at Aldershot in midweek, here I am back in the No. 9 shirt for AFC Bournemouth against Watford in October 1973. I scored the only goal of the game against the Hornets at Dean Court and ended the 1973/74 season as the club's leading scorer. (AFC Bournemouth)

Reunited with my 1974/75 Aldershot teammate Malcom Crosby at the Recreation Ground many years later. (Author's collection)

Looking forward to the new challenge ahead as youth-team coach at Norwich City. (Author's collection)

With the Canaries in China. I'm the one trying to keep cool at the back, whilst manager John Bond (front left) obliges the photographer with a smile. (Author's collection)

Still in China, but this time showing off my 'Hollywood look!' (Author's collection)

With the management team at Manchester City (left to right): coach Glyn Pardoe, assistant manager John Benson, manager John Bond, myself and physiotherapist Roy Bailey. (Author's collection)

Our first Christmas upon moving to Manchester was spent in a hotel together with both the Bond and Benson families but look who got the job of cooking dinner! (Author's collection)

replay and I think they sensed that the advantage had shifted towards Spurs.

Nonetheless, to have finished 12th in the First Division and reach the cup final represented a good first season in charge and, while the chairman looked to spend some of the money that had been brought in on redeveloping the ground, Bondy also had some spending in mind.

Martin O'Neill joined from Norwich for £275,000 and John's son, Kevin, having left Norwich, moved from Seattle Sounders in a deal worth £350,000. But it was the fee of more than £1m paid to Nottingham Forest for England forward Trevor Francis that September that set pulses raising at Maine Road. John was delighted and expected Francis to be the first of several major incoming transfers that season.

We had an excellent pre-season and once the new league season got under way, we started well and challenged near the top of the table. The arrival of Francis had brought speculation that Dennis Tueart would be leaving Maine Road but that was not in John's mind. Instead, he changed our style of play slightly, which appeared to suit Dennis, and he and Trevor seemed to complement each other up front. They were certainly both quality players and Francis scored two goals on his debut at Stoke, but he then picked up an injury during a 4-0 win against Leeds and this kept him out for six weeks.

Before long, a growing injury list included Francis, Paul Power and Gerry Gow and this prompted John to bring Asa Hartford back to Maine Road for a second spell, with Everton receiving £350,000 in return. By now, City's name was cropping up when any player was made available at any price, but the club really couldn't afford to spend any more money. Two players John did still try to buy, though, were Joe Jordan and Justin Fashanu, but both deals fell through at the last minute. To try and recoup some of the cash already paid out, Dave Bennett moved to Cardiff and loyal servant Tommy Booth went to Preston. Earlier in the season, Steve MacKenzie and Tony Henry had also left and more departures were to follow.

With Francis back in action, we moved up to seventh, just five points off surprise league leaders Swansea, before Tueart's season ended when he snapped an Achilles tendon in a 3-2 defeat at home to Sunderland in December. In the next game, though, we beat Liverpool 3-1 on Boxing Day at Anfield, City's first win there for 28 years, and then, in the last game of 1981, we beat Wolves at a packed Maine Road to go top of the First Division.

Looking back, this was a pivotal moment for both John and the club, but one which neither was able to build upon. We were probably two players short of having a side that could sustain a championship bid but, due to heavy spending in the Malcolm Allison era, the money had now run out and, instead, the club's policy was to sell rather than strengthen. John did bring in 34-year-old former Norwich full-back John Ryan on a free transfer from Sheffield United as a back-up for the right-back spot, but after a 3-1 home defeat in the FA Cup against Coventry, Gerry Gow left, joining Rotherham for £75,000.

Martin O'Neill's short stay at Maine Road ended when he returned to Norwich for £125,000, while Phil Boyer and Tommy Hutchison both moved to Bulova in Hong Kong as the wage bill was trimmed. Our home form remained good for a while and kept us in with a shout of a top-three finish, but John was becoming increasingly frustrated and, after a 1-0 defeat against West Ham at the beginning of April, he let the players have it in the dressing room and imposed extra training as punishment for their poor performance.

The wheels certainly seemed to be falling off the cart as we then lost 5-0 at home to Liverpool and, after further defeats against Wolves and Swansea, we were facing a mid-table finish. As a result, the end of the season became a bit of a damp squib and we eventually finished the season in tenth position on 55 points.

City did take part in one moment of English football history during the 1981/82 season, however, when we were involved in the first domestic match in a major competition in England to be decided by penalty kicks. After a 2-2 draw against Stoke City in the second round of the League Cup, it took 20 penalties to decide who would progress in the competition, Joe Corrigan eventually saving one to give City a 9-8 success.

Rumours about the club's financial difficulties continued during the summer of 1982 and as the new stand took shape at Maine Road, Trevor Francis found himself on his way to Italy. The chairman felt that Francis missed rather too many games through injury and the club could no longer afford to pay such high wages for such a player. As a result, Francis joined Sampdoria for £700,000.

John Bond felt let down and I shared his disappointment on losing a thoroughbred, if injury-prone, player who was quick of thought and feet. We weren't the only ones to feel disappointed. Many supporters thought that Trevor had been sold to put a roof on the stand and, when the new season began, attendances plummeted by almost 8,000.

West Ham's David Cross and Southampton's Graham Baker had joined us, and Cross scored in both the season's opening two games. In the next game against promoted Watford at Maine Road, we lost goalkeeper Joe Corrigan with a dislocated shoulder in only the third minute. As the other two Johns looked at me for ideas about who should go in goal, for some reason I suggested that full-back Bobby McDonald should take over. For the next 87 minutes, McDonald performed brilliantly to keep a clean sheet while, at the other end of the pitch, substitute Tueart headed the only goal of the game in his first match back since his Achilles injury. The following day, the *Daily Mail* summed up McDonald's performance between the sticks: 'McDonald managed to look terrified, ham-fisted, courageous and totally unbeatable.' That was about right and it turned out to be one of my better decisions!

I was delighted as well for Dennis to score after he had been through a lengthy rehabilitation to recover from his injury. A true professional, he was extremely popular at the club and I found him a great player to work with. He was a very positive influence in the dressing room, too, but I soon found out he was not one to upset. I have mentioned previously about the drinking culture at my various clubs and Manchester City was no exception. Most teams had a few crates of beer on the coach for the homeward journey on away trips, but at City it was mainly wine. But it had to be the best wine because, if it wasn't, Dennis would create hell, so I made sure it was always the best!

With Corrigan out, 20-year-old Alex Williams took over in goal for the next match. Alex had made his debut the previous year, when he became the first black goalkeeper to play in the First Division.

His first game back ended in a 1-0 defeat at Notts County, but this was followed by a 2-1 win against Spurs, in which

Graham Baker netted twice. Sadly, Williams received a lot of abuse from supporters at the start of the game, but I'm pleased to say that by the end his performance had won over the crowd and he received a good ovation.

Alex again performed well during a 4-1 defeat at West Ham in late September, saving a penalty in a game which saw both Kevin Bond and Asa Hartford sent off. The young goalkeeper was certainly not responsible for our dip in form that left us in ninth position. John continued to try and add to his squad with the limited money he had available and made bids for veteran Nottingham Forest midfielder Archie Gemmill, Southampton full-back Ivan Golac and Ipswich forward Eric Gates. Each bid failed and behind the scenes the club took increasing steps to reduce City's expenditure.

One day, the chairman bumped into me in the corridor and started to ask me a lot of questions about who did what within the team management set-up. I should have put two and two together, but I didn't think too much about it at the time and it came as a shock when the following month John Bond told me that, for some reason, Mr Swales had decided there were too many staff at the top with the first team and wanted to trim the numbers. The idea was that John, along with John Benson, would do the coaching, leaving me surplus to requirements. I could tell he was upset by the decision, but he was not allowed to make any comment publicly.

I have my own thoughts on why this happened and a major factor was that the chairman could not get on with John Bond. Mr Swales had always been 'Mr Manchester City', but now John, such a flamboyant and charismatic character, had taken that role from him. I truly believe, to this day, that Mr Swales wanted to get rid of John but, with the team still doing well, that would have been impossible.

I have a theory that he felt that, by getting rid of me, it would weaken the management team's strength, resulting in more pressure on two rather than three personnel, and thus eventually give him enough ammunition to get rid of the two remaining Johns.

My contract still had another 18 months to run but I was now apparently surplus to requirements, so, never one to cause a fuss, I was gone the next day. A good friend of mine, Mick Brown, the former Manchester United assistant manager, heard of my dismissal and invited me round to his house to commiserate and we polished off a good bottle of brandy between us!

Just before I left, City sat at the top of the league, but they could not sustain their early success as the season progressed. The atmosphere within the club continued to deteriorate. John Bond resigned after an embarrassing cup defeat at Brighton the following February and City were relegated at the end of the season. Prior to John's departure, the worst position City had held was mid-table, but once he left, the club went into freefall.

John later explained that he went to Manchester City because he thought it was bigger than Norwich, but I think he regretted it later. I would say that he was a true inspiration for me as a coach and I feel that I owe a great deal to him. Our philosophy was much the same and he knew he could rely on me to do what he wanted without constant interference. I carried his influence, together with the philosophy of Bill Nicholson, along with me throughout the rest of my career. With those two men as my mentors, I had everything I needed to take my coaching career forward.

Ironically, the curse of 'The Saint' had struck again, though, just as when I had been a player at Reading, Bournemouth and Aldershot and a coach at Norwich, Manchester City were relegated within a year of my leaving!

In the words of Dennis Tueart

'John Sainty was a great help to me as a coach after my return to Manchester City from New York Cosmos, when we had a large amount of young and inexperienced players in the squad along with a few experienced ones. His understanding of the capabilities in the training sessions of both sets of players was excellent and he always made the sessions extremely enjoyable, as well as appropriate to everyone's skills.

'He was a particular help to me when I had ruptured my Achilles tendon. He was constantly talking and encouraging me throughout my rehabilitation programme, and after my plaster had been removed, recommended special exercises and routines to develop the weakened parts of my leg.

'I can only say his communication skills were first class with a strong emphasis on understanding the particular requirement for the player he was dealing with.'

In the words of Joe Corrigan

'As a coach, John Sainty was one of the best, full of good ideas which he put across well. We became friends and got on fantastically. He had a great sense of humour and really involved himself with the players. He was a major influence in getting us to the FA Cup Final in 1981, when sadly we lost to Spurs in the replay.

'Most of all, though, he was a really nice man and a really good friend.'

Joe Corrigan made his first-team debut for Manchester City in 1967 and went on to make 476 league appearances for City during a 17-year career. Capped nine times at full international level by England, he also made league outings for Brighton & Hove Albion, Norwich City and Stoke City.

In the words of Kevin Reeves

'I was delighted to link up with Saint again at Manchester City when John Bond brought him and John Benson there from Norwich. It was very much as it was before and we had two fantastic seasons there that I will never forget.'

In the words of physiotherapist Roy Bailey

'I was the physiotherapist for Manchester City Football Club over many years, working under many different managers. It was fair to say that City changed their managers on a regular basis in a bid to find success. In October 1980, another new one arrived in John Bond, along with John Benson as assistant manager and a coach I had never heard of called John Sainty.

'As soon as these three arrived at Maine Road, things changed immediately, and the path of the football club went from losing to winning on a regular basis. The atmosphere within the club also changed and a lot of this, in my opinion, was down to John Sainty. He brought humour, excitement, trust and loyalty within the framework of the playing staff, something that had been lost for a while.

'I was fortunate to be the person that worked closely with Saint. Over the first two or three months, he and I became very good friends, spending a lot of time working closely together. Quite a bit of our leisure time was also spent together. It was fair to say that Saint liked a little tipple. I recall his drink was vodka and orange, and normally when he got a few of these inside him he would find a nice quiet place inside or outside the house and fall asleep.

'During the day, he worked extremely hard with the players. He was fair but demanded their respect and it was great fun to be with working with him at the football club. He became my room partner for away trips with the club and I knew from the start it would be great fun to be around him.

'Saint enjoyed his job coaching the players. It's always down to the manger when success arrives. However, I put City's immediate success down to the fantastic work that was done with the players by Saint. They loved working with him and, of course, in the first year City got to the 100th FA Cup Final at Wembley. Although we eventually lost to Tottenham in the replay, it was a great testament to the work that Saint did that we got there in the first place.

'Like many thousands of true City fans, I will always fondly remember the time the three Johns spent together at Maine Road. So, many thanks Messrs Bond, Benson and Sainty.'

8.

TRICKY TIMES AT CHESTER AND BURNLEY

A MONTH or so after I had left Maine Road, one of the Manchester City directors recommended me to Chester, who had been relegated from the Third Division at the end of the 1981/82 season and were looking for a manager after long-serving Cliff Sears had stepped down. I took over initially as caretaker coach before being appointed permanently as manager by the chairman, Eric Barnes.

My caretaker role lasted into mid-January 1983. I was quite content with the way things were going, as were the chairman and directors. Mr Barnes was pleased at how both the players and supporters had responded to my appointment, and to my new techniques of coaching and tactics. He appreciated what I was trying to do and offered me the manager's position on a permanent basis. I accepted his offer of the job, but in the back of my mind was something John Bond once said to me. He told me that he did not think I would ever be good enough to be a successful manager, although he saw me as an excellent coach.

Anyway, I applied myself with all the professionalism I could muster, working long hours, and my time at Chester was not all bad, but it did not work out quite as I hoped it might. After stepping down from the manager's role, Cliff Sears stayed on to assist me and one of my everlasting memories from my time at Sealand Road was having the honour to work with him. He was an absolute gem of a human being, too nice to be involved at a football club.

I put forward some ideas of how I felt the club should be run going forward and all of these seemed to be warmly embraced by all concerned. The chairman seemed particularly impressed with my work with the younger players in the team, always something I had enjoyed right from my Spurs days, but as I began my managership on a permanent basis, I had some huge decisions to make, as I was aware that the wage bill needed to be eased.

There was a good bunch of players to work with including Trevor Storton, Paul Manns and Steve Ludlam. Trevor and midfielder Steve Ludlam were the only players in the team who were over the age of 23 and my hope was to base the following season's team around Trevor, as he was such a reliable defender. My ideas of building up a more successful team were to be thwarted, however, as financial problems hit the club and resulted in a very restricted budget being imposed by the board of directors. Welsh youth internationals Mike Williams and John Allen were allowed to go out on loan to Chelsea with the hope of a permanent transfer at the end of the loan period, whilst Steve Ludlam was allowed to join a Finnish league side.

My time with Chester was not all bad and I led the club to a mid-table finish in the Fourth Division and to the semi-finals of the Football League Trophy. The future of the club was dependent on minimal spending and I was told to cut the wage bill at the end of the season, losing two members of my coaching staff in Jim Walker and Vince Prichard as a result, together with the previous season's leading goalscorer, John Thomas, who joined Lincoln City.

Most of the players who remained were non-contract and obviously we really needed to strengthen the side. I had high hopes of bringing in one of my former youngsters at Norwich, Peter Mountford, and of persuading John Fashanu to join us, but unfortunately Peter decided to join Charlton Athletic and John was retained by Norwich. However, I was able to bring in future Welsh international Andy Holden and full-back Lee Dixon, who had been given a free transfer by Burnley. These were early days in Lee's career, but it was easy to see he had ability and ambition. Of course, he went on to better things with Arsenal and England and is still regularly seen on television as a football pundit. John Ryan also agreed to join us. Having worked with him at both Norwich and Manchester City, I was delighted to have him on board. John was a good lad, an honest worker who would give nothing less than his very best.

Nonetheless, the problems of working under a restricted budget were bound to come along to bite me at some point and the 1983/84 campaign started miserably for the newly renamed Chester City. I had a brilliant relationship with the supporters' club and they did their utmost to try and help in every way possible, but the bottom line was that every penny spent by the football club had to be accounted for.

We had arranged a fundraising day during the summer, soon after Manchester United had won that season's FA Cup. At the time, my son, Mark, was playing football in the same team as the son of the United assistant manager, Mick Brown, and it was arranged for the cup to be taken along and displayed at the fundraiser.

It was brought to our house to be kept safely in the airing cupboard overnight, but before that the kids wanted their photos taken with it in the back garden. Naturally, this caused great excitement and somehow the jungle drums started! All of the street seemed to get wind of it and everyone turned up at our house to take photos. I don't think this would happen today. I have no idea how the news got out, but a good guess would be the kids telling their friends at school!

We also wanted to get supporters' club members more involved on matchdays, so much was tried, but with just one league win to our name by November, the writing was on the wall. There was one highlight, however, and that came when we overturned a 3-0 first-leg deficit to knock out Bolton Wanderers in the first round of the League Cup, or Milk Cup as it had then become known.

Goals from Andy Holden, Peter Zelem and Trevor Phillips levelled the tie at Sealand Road before we triumphed in the shoot-out, with penalties scored by Peter Zelem and John Allen, and goalkeeper Phil Harrington emerging as the hero, saving three Wanderers penalties. Then, in the second round, we won 1-0 at Leeds before sadly losing the second leg 4-1 at home in front of a crowd of more than 8,000.

I sensed my time was coming to an end as we dropped to the bottom of the league and, in November 1983, it came during a training session in the gym. I was playing head tennis with Paul Needham, Peter Zelem and Steve Ludlam, who had returned to the club after six months in Finland, when suddenly I was called out from the session and informed that my services were no longer required. I went back to the gym afterwards and apologised to the lads for not being able to finish the game but explained that I had just been sacked!

The following year, the 'Curse of the Saint' struck again, I'm afraid, and Chester City finished the 1983/84 season bottom of the Fourth Division – although, thankfully, they successfully applied for re-election.

After a year at Chester, mug that I was, I was again looking for work. John Bond had taken over at Burnley the previous June and, with the club having been newly relegated to the Third Division, there were high expectations of them going straight back up. But things were not going too well. Bondy was the first manager Burnley had appointed who had not played for them previously and there was a certain amount of negativity towards his appointment. He then upset the applecart further by not re-engaging the previous caretaker manager and former Clarets player, Frank Casper, nor his assistant Gordon Clayton, preferring to bring in his own backroom staff, including John Benson as assistant manager.

Bondy and I had remained in touch after we parted company at Manchester City and whilst I was at Chester. I had, of course, been pleased to pick up Lee Dixon after John informed me that he was prepared to let him go. He also sold the popular Brian Laws to Huddersfield for £10,000 whilst making a number of changes to the playing squad upon his arrival at Turf Moor. The Burnley way had been to produce their own players rather than buying in and it was a system that had, until recently, served them well. But John brought in a lot of players including several from Manchester City. Somehow, he persuaded Kevin Reeves to drop down two divisions and got him for £100,000. Other former City players who came on board included Steve Daley, Willie Donnachie, Gerry Gow, Tommy Hutchison and Dennis

Tueart. But there was lot of turmoil going on behind the scenes, results were not matching expectations and the team ended up finishing the season in 12th place.

I went in to help out by coaching the youngsters there. However, whilst enjoying the coaching, I did not get quite as much pleasure from the other chores John lined up for me. It was perhaps no surprise that cutting the grass at the training pitches and cleaning the dressing rooms, especially during the summer when everyone was away on holiday, left me feeling so fed up that I decided enough was enough. I left a message for John when he returned from holiday saying that he would have to do without me and, basically, I did a runner! John also departed before the start of the following season and Benno took over as manager. You probably won't be surprised to learn that Burnley were another of my former teams to be relegated the following year.

In the words of Chas Sumner, Chester City club historian

'When John was appointed at Chester in November 1983, he was faced with the unenviable task of managing a club at one of its lowest ebbs with severe financial constraints affecting many decisions that were made.

'The second half of the 1970s had seen the club go through one of their most successful periods, finishing fifth in Division Three and reaching the fifth round of the FA Cup on two occasions. However, the tide had turned at the start of the 1980s and Chester were relegated to Division Four at the end of the 1981/82 campaign after finishing well adrift from the pack. The downturn on the pitch not only led to falling attendances but unsuccessful transfer signings on higher wages and high interest rates on a new stand meant that the club were haemorrhaging money.

'The 1982/83 season had started with former youth-team coach Cliff Sears in charge. Cliff was the man who had discovered Ian Rush and Chester had sold the youngster to Liverpool for £300,000 in 1980. However, Cliff had grown increasingly uncomfortable in the role as manager and resigned in November to return to his role with the youth team.

'John was thrown in at the deep end with an FA Cup tie against non-league Northwich Victoria where Chester were defeated after a replay. League victories against Hartlepool, Bristol City and Tranmere saw John's trial period extended before he was confirmed as manager in April with Chester in mid-table. Under the circumstances, 13th position was a respectable achievement given the financial economies which had seen John lose two members of his coaching staff.

'For the 1983/84 season, the newly renamed Chester City faced even deeper financial problems. Leading scorer John Thomas was sold to Lincoln while another eight players were released as the wage bill was slashed in half. Meanwhile, opportunities to sign new players were severely limited, although one of them, Andy Holden, went on to play for Wales. It was a measure of how difficult the situation had become by the fact that two players, Paul Raynor and Trevor Phillips, re-joined the club after being released when Chester had been relegated in 1982.

'When the new season started, John had to rely heavily on non-contract players in order to field a team but, nonetheless, he was able to mastermind the two notable Milk Cup victories against Leeds and Bolton. But, in the league, a season of struggle was inevitable and with only one league win in the first 13 games, John was relieved of his duties with Chester bottom of Division Four. It must be remembered, though, that John had taken over a club on a downward spiral and it was no reflection on him that he had failed to halt the slide with so many factors out of his control affecting the club.'

In the words of John Allen

'I always remember when we first met John because we weren't used to many southerners up in Chester at the time! He came in as caretaker coach and stayed for the rest of the season. As he had previously worked in the First Division with John Bond at Norwich and Manchester City, me and all the other players were more than happy to see him walk in.

'He brought new ideas, big changes in training and a new look to the club. As a young, 18-year-old player, I personally found it great to work with him. He took time to speak with players, treated everyone with respect, and his personal touch was excellent.

'John helped me a lot, but unfortunately the club was going through some very hard times, which made it difficult for a new coach to come in. Personally, I had an excellent relationship with him as far as a young player could have with a head coach. I will always remember his smile and positive attitude in everything he tried to teach and coach us. At the same time, he could be very detailed and demanding but I have very good memories of my short time under John.'

John Allen made 79 Football League appearances for his hometown club Chester between 1981 and 1984. After a brief spell at Mansfield Town, he emigrated to Finland, where he played a further 282 games, serving four different clubs and twice won Finnish championship medals. After his playing career, he remained in Finland, where he moved into coaching and management.

In the words of John Ryan

'I knew Saint from our young days in London in the mid-1960s. He was making a name for himself as a goalscoring youngster in Tottenham's youth-team and even more so in their reserves. I had just signed professional forms for Arsenal, so we heard news from down the road as we met and played in our respective teams. I remember he was a proper handful. I think at this time, Saint was a "man child". He was of a big build and very strong while I was the opposite, not yet finished growing, and I remember thinking "this guy is from a different planet!"

I don't know why he didn't go on to establish himself in the Spurs first team after such a good start and winning England youth honours. At the back of my mind, I wondered if he had become too big, bulky big, and perhaps not so mobile as when he was terrorising defenders just a few years before?

'John was a year and a bit older than me and our careers took different paths, but I think we played against each other a couple of times when he was at Reading and maybe once at Bournemouth when I was doing seven years at Luton Town. That was it then until I signed for Norwich City and we met up again.

'He was a terrific coach, inspirational in as much that his training sessions were informative, simply delivered and fun. It was a great time to come to work. We were certainly punching our weight, if not exceeding it at times. We had a happy group of players and staff in which Saint played an integral part with his quick sense of humour and one-line answers in the hullabaloo that is a football dressing room.

'I can't say we were close friends, but we were close workmates within the management/worker divide that there must be in a professional football club.

'There must be a divide between managers, coaches and physios but it was never a problem. I enjoyed his company both at work and on the few occasions we met socially … no stories really to tell you, I'm afraid!

'John called me when he was managing at Chester and I went across and played four games for him, but I was nearly 37 and past my best, and the team wasn't good enough to carry me around! I soon told him and he knew, obviously, that I wasn't going to be able to help him out and we parted company on good terms.

'I bumped into him for the last time in the late 1990s when he was at Southampton and I had to deliver coaching courses to the club's apprentices for the PFA. Soon after this, I moved out to Spain. You don't need me to tell you what a good lad he was. I enjoyed my times with him and certainly at Norwich he helped me on to the best spell of my career.'

John Ryan was predominantly a full-back, but he could also play in midfield and enjoyed a professional playing career that lasted more than 20 years. He had spells at eight different Football League clubs and made more than 500 appearances. He also played in the United States.

In the words of Kevin Reeves

'Finally, Saint and I linked up at Burnley with John Bond and Saint again played a pivotal part in my career, though not through coaching, but by him leaving the club. Unfortunately, at

26 years of age, I had to retire through injury halfway through the season. I had absolutely no idea what I was going to do and had two years left on my contract.

'Saint had been taking the reserve and youth teams, but I think having previously been involved with first-team players for so long, he decided to leave the role and the club. With this position now vacant, John Bond offered the role to myself and Tommy Hutchison and, through that experience, I decided I really loved coaching and took all my coaching qualifications with the FA.

'I ended up coaching at different levels for 20 years and then scouting for a further 14. In a strange way, my longevity in the game was down to Saint. He played a massive part in my career at all my playing clubs but much more important was the fact he was a lovely, lovely fella.'

9.
THE PUB LANDLORD

SO, WHAT to do next?

Ever since my Bournemouth days, I had always done part-time jobs like painting and cleaning to help keep busy during the summer, so I had some experience to fall back on. Not surprisingly then, I decided to get a pub! I became landlord of the Railway Inn, Hyde Road, Woodley, Cheshire. On reflection, not the best of ideas, although I stuck at it for seven years, during which time I also became a Class Three referee and was persuaded to become manager of non-league sides Armthorpe Welfare, Glossop North End and Mossley – also not the best of ideas!

I obtained my referee's badges to officiate in Division Eight of the Stockport League. On matchdays, you changed in the car, otherwise you had to get undressed with the players!

In March 1987, I went to Mossley and at the time they were struggling in the Northern Premier League. Neil Wilson, who had coached with me at Chester and Glossop was a good and loyal friend, and he came in with me. We managed to finish the season in tenth place, but the next season didn't start off too well and I stepped down in October as I thought I was letting good people at the club down. I found it so difficult to go from training full-time professionals six days a week to these lads who were only able to spare two or three evenings for a couple of hours at a time and, as much as I tried, I didn't feel able to get the best out of them. This was probably because, in all fairness, my heart wasn't in it. The players even had to leave their car headlights on so that we could see the pitch when we trained!

Throughout my career as a coach, I likened a group of players to a symphony orchestra with myself as the conductor. If the conductor is not able to give 100 per cent, how could the players be expected to do so? When performing well, an orchestra will all learn their individual skills; cellist, violinist, drummer, etc. All these individual skills combine to complete the musical presentation and a football team is no different. The players will all learn their individual skills, then combine to try and make their team better than the opposition.

In both cases, one individual not knowing their role will put everything off balance. In contrast, if everyone knows what to do and when to attempt to do it, he or she makes it easier for their fellow musicians or team-mates. Both need structure and the discipline to play as a totally solid unit.

As a coach or conductor, you have to be quick to discover an individual's strengths and weaknesses and to assess what those give your team. My philosophy was to first try and improve a player's strengths, to make sessions enjoyable and to praise individuals and teams rather than get them to immediately try things that would not in any way improve their overall standards. Nor would I ask them to play in a way that they would not be comfortable with. Instead, I would focus my attention at a later stage on the points that needed correction.

But for now, it seemed that football had had enough of me and me of it, for the time being at least.

Pub life was something I enjoyed at first and although back then opening hours were not all day as they are now, there was always a great deal to do. I also bought a dog, a standard poodle that we named Henry, and he was quite a handful. He became a fearsome guard dog and I would take him for his walks up on the viaduct, which was above the pub. Our living quarters were not exactly spacious, with both children still at school. Joanna was by now at drama school and this meant a lot of ferrying to and fro.

Although the pub opening hours were set, I decided that I would open up one hour earlier for the footballers of the local pub teams, as long as they entered via the back door. This went down well with the players and hopefully it did not affect their play too much!

The pub kitchen was too small to provide hot food as such but, because I have always loved cooking, I devised my own speciality and on Saturdays I would make 'railway pie'. This was a variation on cottage pie, with the addition of black pudding, which always went down a storm and quickly ran out. So good was it, that some of my locals would ask if any was left to take home.

Then, on Sunday afternoons, I served up my other speciality, chip baguettes! The pie and those legendary baguettes were the only food I did serve, but both were immensely popular and some of my old customers still mention them whenever I see them today. The regulars were a nice crowd who rarely caused me any problems, although on one occasion I had to talk down a 'jumper', who had a bad day, from the railway viaduct.

Whilst I was involved in all this and keeping really busy, I received a phone call out of the blue from Eric Webster, who was then manager at Stockport County. He asked if I could possibly help him out by coaching the first team on a part-time basis.

Apparently, a good friend of mine called Brian Cowburn, who was secretary at Mossley, had mentioned my name to Eric and I jumped at the opportunity. I was on my way back to where I belonged.

In the words of Brian Cowburn, former club secretary of Mossley FC

'John resigned in October 1987 after a 3-0 FA Trophy defeat at Alfreton, saying he felt he was letting good people down. It was not the case, of course, but a typically honest response from John.

'He and I became good mates and some years later he got me into scouting for Southampton, which I carried out for six years.

'So many good memories and I was delighted to be present at John's second marriage to Lindsay in Edinburgh.'

In the words of Tony Bugby

'I remember John as if it was only yesterday. He was an extremely likeable individual and his knowledge of football was extraordinary. As a coach, he had a great reputation in the game.

'When he was managing Mossley, I used to either ring him on the landline at the Railway Inn or drop in for the latest news. John had a fairly hopeless task with no funds; therefore, leaving the club was hardly his fault.'

Tony Bugby reported on Mossley FC for the *Oldham Evening Chronicle*.

In the words of Andy Birchenough

'First of all, I feel very privileged to write a piece for this wonderful book as John was a wonderful gentleman and a good friend who I knew for a number of years inside and outside of football.

'I first got to know Saint when he was landlord of my local pub, the Railway Inn in Woodley. It was at this time when my grandparents, Charlie and Jean Kirk, and my own parents, Paul and Ann Birchenough, used to class The Railway as their local and as a family we used to go in on a Sunday afternoon, where we would find Saint behind the bar with that great smile he always had on his face.

'At that time, I was only young and I was told all about how good Sunday afternoons were there and I got talking to Saint about football. At the time, I did not know he was involved with Stockport County and, as the conversation got going, I was really getting excited about what he had to say about what was happening at the club. Please bear in mind that this was when County were not at the top of the league and winning any major honours but, nonetheless, as a child, it thrilled me no end.

'By the way, the chip baguettes that Saint served up there on Sunday afternoons were also an absolute treat to me and others in the pub!

'Moving forwards 12 months later to 1989, my father took me to my first game at Edgeley Park and we sat in the main stand [the Danny Bergara Stand]. As we watched the players warm up before the game, I mentioned to him that I recognised the man who was taking charge. It was Saint and, as chance would have it, he came across for a chat and he remembered me from the Railway Inn and I, of course, had instantly recognised him. I said to him that I never thought he was a coach at County and he explained that he didn't like to big himself up by saying so in the pub and, for that reason, I was in awe of him.

'It set me thinking and I worked out that Saint had actually been involved in football for quite a while. A few months later, when Danny Bergara came from Rochdale as manager, I went to watch a pre-season friendly being played at Woodley Sports. Saint saw me stood by the dugouts and instantly came over and asked if I would be interested in meeting the players afterwards and I, of course, replied "Yes, please!" This was when my journey as a Stockport County fan really began and I was hooked in. Saint, along with Danny and the players, made me so welcome and I will always be grateful to Saint for taking the time to welcome me whenever we saw each other.

'A really big thank you Saint for being such a kind gentleman both in and out of football. I will always be grateful for everything you did for me.'

Andy Birchenough remains a die-hard Stockport fan to this day and, after John moved on, he and Andy continued their friendship.

In the words of another County fan, Robert Walton

'I knew John from the Railway pub. He was a great guy. A few years later, I took my son to watch County at Blackpool. After the game, the team bus was outside the ground and John was stood next to it, so I went up to him and asked him if he could get my son some autographs. He took us on to the bus and told all the players to give my son, Robb, their autographs. John wasn't happy with the team because they had lost and he wanted them to repay Robb for travelling. It is a great memory we will never forget.

'Thank you, John. RIP'

10.

LESSONS IN LIFE WITH DANNY BERGARA

SO, HERE I was with a good bunch of lads who all worked hard and, with Eric Webster's way of dealing with things, there was never any pressure put on me. The lads could enjoy their football and it was a pleasure to go into Edgeley Park to work.

After doing the rounds in non-league football, Eric worked his socks off for Stockport County, seven days a week. He started off as groundsman before becoming assistant manager to Jimmy McGuigan and eventually took charge himself in 1982. It was a far from easy job and County persistently struggled near the foot of the Fourth Division and had to seek re-election at the end of the 1984/85 season.

Eric was dismissed but what you have to bear in mind, though, was that Eric was not only manager, but at times also assistant manager, coach, scout, kit man and groundsman, so he was understandably finding things a little difficult!

By then, either Eric had fallen out of love with Stockport or they had done so with him. I was never sure which and it seemed that nobody really cared. There is little sentiment in football and, in the end, you are just a statistic. Nonetheless, he returned to his previous role as groundsman.

I carried on helping out at County as they went through four different managers – Colin Murphy (twice), Les Chapman, Jimmy Melia and former Manchester City midfielder Asa Hartford before a new chairman, Brendan Elwood, came in. He and the board of directors took the decision to appoint 46-year-old Danny Bergara in March 1989. Danny had previously been in charge at Rochdale for just seven months and had the distinction of being one of the first overseas managers appointed by a Football League club.

Born in Uruguay, Bergara had played in Spanish soccer after moving to that country as a teenager. Eventually, he carved out a coaching career for himself in England and it was Harry Haslam who first employed him at Luton. When Haslam moved to Sheffield United, he took Danny along and made him his assistant. Later, Danny had a spell as caretaker boss at Bramall Lane before moving on to Rochdale.

Our paths had never crossed before, but I was introduced to Danny by Eric, who explained to him my role at the club and Danny asked me to stay on for a couple of weeks, just to show him around and explain the club's workings. Meanwhile, he brought in Brian Green as his assistant, who had been with him at Rochdale, which left me wondering if I would still have a job at the end of this. The manager's office at Edgeley Park was in a basement off the main corridor and quite pokey, with only two desks, one for the manager and one for the assistant, so Brian and I had one desk to share! However, we were able to get by and the three of us seemed to get on well together. After six weeks, Danny had still been unable to decide who he wanted as his assistant but, luckily for me, Brian had by then made the decision to leave, so Danny did not have to make a choice in the end.

By then, Brendan and Danny had begun to turn around the fortunes of the club on and off the pitch. Fourth Division survival was ensured at the end of the 1988/89 season. Danny took full control over players and coaching staff and, although money was tight, he had a good rapport with Brendan and most of the directors, who were all travelling from their homes in Sheffield, as was Danny.

The build-up to the 1989/90 season saw a big clear-out and at one point the club had only eight registered players on its books. Danny then brought in his replacements, with four players coming from his previous club, Rochdale, including player-coach Paul Jones. Another former player of his, the vastly experienced 32-year-old striker Keith Edwards, arrived from Sheffield United.

Edwards hit the ground running and scored four goals in his first six games, while Brett Angel, one of the 'Stockport Eight', was also finding the net regularly. By the end of October, County had reached the top of the Fourth Division table. By Christmas, we had slipped back to fifth and Danny went back to Bramall Lane to sign a young central defender called Jim Gannon, who would remain at the club for ten years and later return as manager.

A superb run towards the end of the season saw County qualify for the play-offs for the first time in the club's history, but the season ended in some disappointment after we suffered a heavy defeat against Chesterfield in the semi-final.

Nonetheless, for a club that had finished no higher than 11th in the Fourth Division in the previous 18 years, it had been a thrilling campaign for all concerned and Danny issued a statement to the club's supporters, promising that we would go up the following season. The chairman and directors were easy to get along with and always open to our ideas. They were usually supportive and I was thoroughly enjoying being back in the world I knew best.

Danny had mainly worked with younger players during his time at Luton and one of his favourite sayings was: 'If the foundations of any building were correct, then the rest of the building would progress and improve.' With this in mind, he wanted to build a good youth set-up at the club. Enter at this point Dave Jones. I had known Dave through my contacts at nearby non-league club Mossley, who recommended him.

As a player, Dave had been a central defender and made around 180 senior appearances in seven years for Everton, the club he had idolised as a lad. He then moved to Coventry but suffered a cruciate ligament injury in his second season at Highfield Road. After a two-year spell at Preston, he had to quit playing at 29 years of age and decided to move into coaching. In addition to his time at Mossley, Dave had also enjoyed considerable success in non-league football with Southport and Morecambe. He came along to Edgeley Park for an interview just before the end of the season, and so began a great working relationship.

Dave initially took on the role of youth-team coach. However, soon afterwards we began to realise Danny wasn't so keen on the youth policy after all and Dave became somewhat frustrated, so Danny decided to make him first-team coach.

Danny had now completed the structure of his new management team – himself as manager, me as his assistant and Dave as first-team coach, together with our kit man, John Bishop, and physio, Rodger Wylde, who had himself previously been a player at Edgeley Park before completing his medical exams.

Pre-season under Danny always began at an army camp somewhere in the south of England to try and build up a good team spirit. The regime would be tough going each day under the direction of army fitness instructors. We would have to tackle obstacle courses and go on seven- or eight-mile runs. As was the case during my own playing days, I could always be found at the rear on these runs, along with the goalkeepers! I have to say, the lads were a terrific bunch to work with, although success always makes things somewhat easier.

Danny proved true to his word when, after 21 years rooted in the bottom tier, County were promoted to the old Third Division at the end of the 1990/91 season. He had lost the services of the previous season's leading goalscorer, Brett Angel, in the close season but had made some crucial signings during the campaign, which included former England youth international winger Andy Kilner, who I had coached as a youngster at Burnley, and 6ft 7in centre-forward Kevin Francis, who cost £45,000 from Derby County. Both players remain hugely loved by Stockport fans.

Our first glimpse of Kevin came when Danny and I took in a reserve game at Derby where this very tall, strong young man stood out and we were desperately keen to bring him to Edgeley Park. Danny and I believed that Kevin was capable of being more than just a targetman in the Fourth Division and the deal was done with the Rams manager, Arthur Cox.

From his first training session, I would get him to start dribbling with the ball, so he could take on seasoned defenders at speed, leaving them on the back foot and wondering just what they were up against. It worked a treat, started to transform his game and Kevin became very hard for opponents to deal with. As well as his attacking prowess, his height came in extremely useful in defensive situations.

Another former Sheffield United player to play a significant part in County's success was big Irishman Paul A. Williams. He had already smashed in 14 goals before a wonderful strike in a 3-0 win against Rochdale earned him a deadline day £250,000 move to Second Division West Bromwich Albion.

Success always makes things somewhat easier, so promotion to the Third Division saw more significant signings, including tough-tackling Rochdale midfielder Peter Ward, and brought a pre-season win against Second Division Port Vale and a draw with 'noisy neighbours' Manchester City. Then, after we had started the 1991/92 season in fine style, Danny was offered a new five-year contract.

Meanwhile, my role was to continue to assist with the coaching and be the organiser, making sure everything was in place for the players, sorting travel to away games, hotel bookings, food and drink on the coach and so on. I wasn't happy that after home games the players tended to go and drink in the supporters' bar and, with the support of the directors, we set up separate players' and directors' bars, which proved a success. I became responsible for the organisation of both bars, ordering in supplies, arranging staff and banking the proceeds, so my previous pub experience proved invaluable, although I managed to push a lot of the work on to my daughter, Joanna.

We took the Third Division by storm, beating Swansea 5–0 on the opening day of the season and quickly became contenders in the race for promotion. In December, Danny signed 24-year-old Wrexham striker Andy Preece for £10,000 and he became the perfect attacking partner for Francis.

We reached Wembley twice in the space of ten days in the play-offs and the Autoglass Trophy, only to lose on both occasions, 2–1 to Peterborough in the play-off final and 1-0 to Stoke in the Autoglass Trophy Final, where Danny became the first manager born outside the British Isles to lead out an English club at Wembley.

Sometimes in football you get the feeling that some things are not meant to be. I felt that after Manchester City's FA Cup Final defeat in 1981 and I felt it again this time with Stockport. In the Autoglass Trophy Final, Kevin Francis had what seemed to be a perfectly good goal disallowed with the score 0-0, while Mark Stein looked suspiciously offside when he struck Stoke's winner. Then, a week later, Ken Charlery's first goal for Peterborough was allowed to stand, even though the ball did not appear to have crossed the line, and Francis then had a goal incorrectly disallowed for offside.

The supporters were undeniably captivated by Danny, his South American dialect and the history behind his move to Stockport. But Dave and I realised quite quickly that he was not the easiest man to deal with.

He was a complete workaholic and didn't take to travelling in from Sheffield each day, so he decided to take digs locally. His first digs were only about 20 yards' walk from the ground and his second digs were no more than a 20-minute walk. He frequently stayed late at the ground as a result and Dave and I frequently had problems getting away, as Danny spent endless hours in the office and expected us to do the same. He seemed to forget that Dave lived in Southport and, although it was not quite so bad for me living just outside Stockport, there were many times we didn't get away before 8pm and sometimes 10pm, so we often felt we were never away from the place. That said, both Dave and I learned an awful lot from Danny, much of it good, some not so good, but the lessons we learned certainly served us well for the future. We used to cringe at some of the things Danny would do, but the game always needs larger-than-life characters and Danny was certainly that. I remember him saying once that he was 'a page short of a genius'; he had read that in a book!

Most of the time, though, his answer to anything and everything asked of him was simply: 'Whatever!' 'What time shall we start training, Danny?' 'Whatever!'

He was capable of unbelievable ball skills in training. His touch and control were brilliant and he could do things with a football that most players would not be able to emulate in their lifetime. His party piece was to toss a coin into the air, catch it on his forehead and, from there, drop it in his top pocket! The trick was brilliant but bear in mind the coin was always borrowed and, at the end of the trick, it would stay firmly in Danny's top pocket!

He was a terror for food and would eat anything. He was certainly not overly concerned about 'use before' dates. I remember he once took some yoghurts out of the fridge which were about nine months past their date and Dave said: 'Danny, you can't eat those, they are way out of date and look awful.' Danny glanced back with a wry smile before leaving the room with the yoghurts. I dared him to eat them but, thankfully, I think he took Dave's advice on this occasion.

Naturally, when Brazilian World Cup star Jairzinho came over to hold a soccer school just down the road from us at Cheadle Town in October 1991, Danny was keen to meet him and suggested to Cheadle chairman Chris Davies that he bring him along to County's home game against Chester. Unfortunately, it was not a good choice, as County lost the game 4-0 and Danny's post-match inquisition went on so long that Jairzinho decided to call it a night and left.

Undeterred, Chris decided to arrange another meeting and suggested the player would like to come down to watch a training session one morning instead. This particular morning dawned cold, wet and windy, a typical Manchester autumn day. At around 11am, Jairzinho strode across to the touchline and I greeted him with a handshake whilst promising Danny would come off the pitch to join us. Try as I might and shouting as much as I could, I was unable to get Danny's attention and he carried on with the session, totally absorbed and completely ignoring me and everyone alongside me. The cold, wind and damp soon proved too much for the Brazilian and he asked Chris if they could leave, so Danny never did get to meet the star, but I, at least, had that pleasure.

Despite a mixed bag of results in the first half of the 1992/93 season, County remained in and around the play-off positions. Later in the season, Paul A. Williams returned from West Brom for a fraction of the fee he was sold for after an unhappy spell at The Hawthorns and was amongst the goalscorers in a 5-1 drubbing of West Brom at Edgeley Park. He was joined at County by a defender named Mike Flynn, who arrived from Preston in a £125,000 deal and was destined to spend a decade at Stockport.

However, a poor run of form towards the end of the season saw us first miss out on automatic promotion, then fall victim to Port Vale in the play-off semi-finals. After scoring 39 goals in all competitions that season, Kevin Francis was suspended from both legs of the semi-final, but he was available two days later for the Autoglass Trophy Final, our third appearance at Wembley in three seasons.

Port Vale were our opponents once more, but the Wembley hoodoo struck again and we found ourselves two goals down at half-time. Big Kevin pulled a goal back in the second half, but Vale hung on to inflict more heartbreak on Danny and the team.

Danny promised he would give the same group of players a second crack at promotion and, apart from goalkeeper Ian Ironside, who joined us from Middlesbrough, he did not add to the squad during the close season ahead of the 1993/94 campaign. After topping the table in November, we had slipped a little by New Year, but victories in the first two rounds of the FA Cup had set us up with a visit from Premier League Queens Park Rangers in the third round.

The game produced one of the side's best performances during Danny's time in charge. Simon Barker put Rangers ahead after 19 minutes but, with a mixture of craft and graft, the players responded by attacking in swarms. There was a certain amount of controversy when Francis equalised 20 minutes later, with team-mate Tony Barras lying injured in an offside position, but there could no complaint about the winning goal, Andy Preece sweeping home a 74th-minute volley to put County in the fourth round of the cup for the first time in 29 years.

Three defeats in our next five games, though, saw us drop out of the FA Cup at the hands of Bristol City, conquerors of Liverpool in the previous round, and also exit the Autoglass Trophy. However, our league form generally remained good and we lost only three of our last 18 games. It was enough to secure a play-off spot with four games remaining but, unfortunately, we failed to turn this into an automatic promotion place on the last day and had to try and lift everybody's spirits in time for a semi-final against York City.

A solitary goal from Chis Beaumont five minutes from the end of the second leg at Edgeley Park settled the tie and we were off to Wembley again, this time to face Burnley, who had finished 12 points behind us. There had been 'previous' between the two clubs in recent years and the Wembley showpiece was not to prove any different, I'm afraid.

Our captain, Peter Ward, was booked in the first minute for a foul on the Clarets' Ted McMinn, but 60 seconds later, Chris Beaumont put us in front when he headed home David Frain's free kick. In the 13th minute, Mick Wallace was sent off by referee David Elleray following a clash with McMinn, after which he was alleged to have spat at him. Burnley equalised through David Eyres just before the half-hour and the teams went off at half-time level at 1-1.

The second half saw the ten men of County still holding firm until Beaumont was dismissed for a foul on Les Thompson in the 61st minute and ten became nine. Four minutes later, Gary Parkinson put Burnley ahead but, even with only nine men, the side kept attacking and almost forced extra time when Andy Preece's shot was only just kept out by the Clarets' goalkeeper, Marlon Beresford.

None of us could condone the behaviour of either Wallace or Beaumont but, having been awarded the fair play trophy for the best disciplinary record in the Second Division, it was ironic that we became the first English side to have two players dismissed at Wembley for foul play.

The 2-1 defeat was another huge disappointment and, unfortunately, this time all was not well behind the scenes.

Preece had enjoyed the most prolific period of his career during his time with County since Danny plucked him from Wrexham's reserve side, scoring 42 goals in 97 league appearances and enjoying a wonderful partnership with Kevin Francis. That summer, he signed for Crystal Palace for £350,000, a testament to Danny's ability to spot talent.

Several new faces arrived, including striker Alun Armstrong from Newcastle United, whilst several of the old guard were allowed to leave. The 18-year-old Armstrong began well and, for a time, the team were challenging near the top as usual, but a slump in form during November heralded a downturn in performances. By January 1995, we had dropped to mid-table, although Francis had maintained his remarkable scoring rate, having already netted 13 goals during the season to take his total with the club to more than 100 in all competitions.

For over a year, his hometown club Birmingham City had been tracking him and manager Barry Fry finally stepped in with an £800,000 offer to take Kevin back down the M6. The offer broke County's record for an outgoing transfer and another financial windfall came about thanks to Danny.

Ian Helliwell was signed from Rotherham United for £20,000 to try and replace Kevin and he scored twice on his debut in a 4-0 win against Hull City. Not surprisingly, though, he could not find the net with the same consistency as someone whose scoring exploits for County had become legendary. During the next few weeks, Dave and I had become frustrated because other teams had worked out our style of play and whenever we tried to suggest a different approach, Danny would not listen.

He simply pointed out that things had gone along pretty well so far and he was not amenable to change. Dave and I could never really work out why, with Danny's skills and his South American roots, his concept of playing football was invariably a long-ball game, always opting for a big striker such as Kevin Francis.

Training sessions had become more bizarre. We were doing four practice matches each week, then every Friday we would play a full-scale training match. This was split into three sessions of 20 minutes each and Danny's focus was on countering whatever way he believed our next opposition would line up. In fact, we seemed to concentrate more on what the opposition were going to do to us rather than what we would do to them.

Mid-March saw a 3-1 win against Crewe Alexandra to mark Danny's sixth anniversary in the manager's chair but by the end of the month he was relieved of his duties as manager following a disagreement between himself and chairman Brendan Elwood. It came as something of a shock to everyone at the club and particularly to the supporters.

Danny always enjoyed a drink, whisky being his favourite tipple, and staying away from home in digs probably encouraged him to drink a little more than he should have at times and, sadly, during the last 18 months of his time as manager, it did become a problem. Dave and I tried to play it down and cover for Danny when we could, but his relationship with the chairman had become strained.

Brendan wanted him to relocate from Sheffield and eventually they had a major falling-out because of Danny's reluctance to do so. Heated words were exchanged after he returned from a game at Plymouth and things got seriously out of hand. Sadly, there was only ever going to be one winner and it was not Danny. Both he and the chairman were very strong characters. Danny later submitted a claim for unfair dismissal and a long, drawn-out case followed.

From my perspective, I had by this time worked with some wonderful people in football, but it was an honour to have known and worked alongside Danny. He was a truly unique human being, good for football and especially good for Stockport County. During his six years in charge, he played a huge part in providing a solid foundation for a once ailing club.

I took away many fine memories and also many amusing ones. Danny's choice of music on away games was something I will always remember. As we set off on our journey, he would get to the front of the coach and we would all know what was to come next. On would go his favourite CD, The Gypsy Kings, as he thought everyone enjoyed it! The problem was, he was probably the only one who actually did. Cries of 'rubbish' and 'get it off' made no difference to him; he was quite oblivious and, after all, he was the manager!

As I have mentioned previously, Danny had some peculiar ways and one of my funniest recollections occurred during a trip to the Isle of Man, where we were taking part in a pre-season tournament. The whole first-team squad travelled, as Danny wanted to win the tournament, which featured some other professional teams alongside some local sides.

Unfortunately, most of the players considered themselves to be on a holiday, but certainly not Danny. He placed a curfew on the players and there was to be no drinking or late nights – they had to be in their rooms by 9pm.

Every evening, Danny would do the rounds, knocking on each door to make sure the players were safely in for the evening.

All the rooms were on the first floor of the hotel, so either the stairs or the lift had to be used to get downstairs. Danny, therefore, decided to station himself on a seat outside the lift for an hour after 9pm each evening. So, if anyone decided to take a chance and try to get out, he would catch them … or so he thought. The players soon found out and a number decided to go out on to their balconies and drop one floor below to get out. Thankfully, no serious injuries occurred.

On another evening when Danny went around checking the players were all present and correct in their rooms, he knocked on one door, I think it was Michael Oliver's room, and called out: 'Who's in there?' He was expecting Michael to reply, but back came the response: 'Michael and Linda.' Imagine Danny's horror! He went mad, but when the rest of us heard the story, we couldn't stop laughing. We saw the funny side, but Danny definitely did not.

During the tournament, there were several question-and-answer sessions arranged with representatives from each of the participating clubs in attendance. The managers and coaching staff were usually present, plus a couple of players. Danny was usually positioned near the front, but Dave and I went along and stood at the back and then, as soon as the session started, we nipped out for a drink in the nearest pub, timing it carefully so we would get back just as it would end. Danny would always ask how we thought it went afterwards and we would emphatically answer: 'Brilliant!'

One particularly loyal County fan came across to watch us during the tournament. He was very short in stature and would be known in today's 'PC' world as a 'little person'. He was a devoted fan and I remember before home games he would run out with the players if he could get away with it and join the captains at the coin toss. If challenged, 'I'm with them!' was his favourite reply. Anyway, he came across to the Isle of Man tournament hiding in the skip with the kit! He was a real character who clearly didn't have much money and the lads all loved him.

Did we win the tournament? Not a cat in hell's chance!

But history shows the success Danny achieved at Edgeley Park and the fact that 'Bergara's Blue and White Army' is still lovingly remembered there today is testimony to his huge personality. Stockport had once again become a well-respected lower league club, but it needed to keep moving forwards and it was now down to Dave and me to fashion things in our own style.

In the words of Danny's wife, Jan Bergara

'Danny and John shared a special respect for each other. They were actually like 'chalk and cheese'. John so laid back and occasionally known to nod off during some of Danny's endless post-match talks when all he wanted to do was get back home, whilst Danny was somewhat extrovert, to say the least. However, I do know how much Danny respected and valued John's steady and reliable input.

'My son, Simon, noticed and acknowledged John at the back of a packed church for Danny's funeral, having travelled all the way up from Southampton to attend. As a family, we've never forgotten how much that meant to us. So, rest in peace John … that is if Danny will allow you to.'

In the words of Steve Bellis

'In Danny Bergara, Dave Jones and John Sainty, we had a perfect trio in football terms at Stockport County. Danny had the passion, dedication and eccentricity at times, Jonesy was the laid back one, but with a disciplined streak, and Saint was, well he was just Saint: knowledgeable, approachable and affable with a great sense of mischief and humour.

'As part of my role as the club's marketing manager, I was tasked with sitting with Danny to write down and decipher his programme notes, which became legendary. This could take up to two hours sat by the great man at his desk and would then involve another couple of hours or so trying to make sense of it all and then deciding just how much was actually printable.

'Bearing in mind how long this could take, I would always try and get into Danny's office early in the afternoon after training. Saint was usually there when I arrived and on far too many occasions when I suggested to Danny that we could do his notes now, Saint would interject with a mischievous grin and chirp: "Wouldn't it be better if Steve came back at about 5pm gaffer?" Danny would immediately respond with: "Yeah, good idea Saint. See you at five, Bello."

'He lived in digs across the road from the ground and was never in a rush to get home, so this always meant a long evening for me, often getting home nearer to 10pm, which Saint found highly amusing. I'll never forget Saint's big smile as I trudged up the stairs from the office each time.

'Saint was very comfortable in the club bars, too, where he put his experience as a licensee to very good use. There weren't many assistant managers who would willingly combine their role with driving the club minibus and managing the club bars, but that was Saint. He gave his all and always with a wry smile.

'He was a dream to work with and an inspiration to many. I loved him dearly, even though he did make me stay late every week to do Danny's notes.'

Steve Bellis was appointed as marketing manager at Stockport County in 1989 after serving as vice-chairman of the official supporters' club during the 1980s. He went on to head up the commercial department from 1996 until 2004. Bellis returned to Edgeley Park as an advisor to the club's board in 2014 and became a club director in 2016. He played a key role in persuading the council to purchase Edgeley Park, protecting its future use for County at a time of uncertainty for the club. Having served the club for more than 40 years, he is currently club president.

In the words of Dave Jones

'Both John and I had the greatest respect for Danny, but that did not stop us playing a few tricks on him! The day before a match, he would always ask us what team he should play and, after a few weeks, we noticed that whatever team we selected, Danny would change it. So, from then on, John and I would select the team that we thought Danny would want to play, knowing that he would have to change it, as we had picked it. That way, more often than not, the outcome was that we would get the team John and I actually wanted!

'He had this thing about everything being in its place on his desk but couldn't understand why things kept moving around. The answer was simple, of course. John was always a bit of a wind-up merchant and, as soon as Danny's back was turned, he would set about repositioning his ornaments and equipment just to see his reaction.

'Danny was nobody's fool, though, as John and I found out when we asked him about a pay rise while we were playing in a tournament over in the Isle of Man. Danny soon agreed to John's request, but mine required a little more negotiation before he offered me an extra £10. I accepted, but when I told John, he pointed out that I had actually taken his money, which had suddenly dropped by the same amount. Danny had taken £10 off John and given it to me!

'Periodically, Danny would have his quirks and on one occasion during a spell of bad results, he brought in a psychologist to talk to the players. She had them in the dressing room chanting repetitively: 'We are the best! We are the best!' It was too much for John and I to keep a straight face and we slipped out to the toilets. Another time, Danny became concerned about the players' diets and brought in a food expert. That lasted until we lost a couple of games and then we returned to normal, and fish and chips was back on the menu, much to John's delight!'

In the words of Rodger Wylde

'John Sainty was an important part of a fantastic backroom staff that chairman Brendan Elwood assembled as a launchpad to take County from perennial revellers at the bottom of the Fourth Division to the dizzy heights of the Championship. The other staple members of that backroom staff were Danny Bergara, Dave Jones and myself, who were there throughout the majority of that wonderful rise up through the leagues.

'It is always difficult to "put a finger" on how to be successful in professional football and there is no certain recipe for success, otherwise every team in the league would be successful, which is impossible. Success at a club just occurs. The right staff, the right players and, most importantly, the right chairman making the correct decisions. This is what happened when Brendan Elwood took over at Stockport County in 1988. He made all the right crucial decisions in every department over the initial 15 years to take us to the Championship.

'Appointing Danny as manager who, in turn, appointed John as his assistant was genius. Saint wasn't a "yes" man by any means. Saint said what he thought in the manager's office, some of which Danny took on board and some of which he did not. This respect for each other's football opinions was vital in making good on-field decisions.

'The respect for Saint that Danny had was no more evident than in half-time team talks. We would all return to the dressing room and the first person to say his piece was Saint, not Danny. There was no pre-talk conclave preparation by the pair. This Saint first, Danny second routine was something that just developed from the outset and developed because of each other's confidence that they were both on the same football song sheet.

'This routine lasted throughout their time together at Edgeley Park and was, I believe, intrinsic in our success as a football club.'

Rodger Wylde played for six Football league clubs during a career that spanned a period of 17 years, the last of which was Stockport County, where he spent the 1988/89 season. In order to stay in football, he took a degree course which enabled him to qualify as a physiotherapist and Danny Bergara brought him back to the club in that capacity. He remained for more than 25 years and served under 11 different managers.

In the words of Paul Jones

'I moved to Stockport County from Rochdale when Danny Bergara became the manager at Edgeley Park. Danny had brought me back to England from South Africa and, when he made the move from Spotland the following year, he offered me a role as player-coach in his new coaching and management staff.

'I will always remember that even though I didn't really know much about the coaching side of things in those early days, Saint was always a great help to me. He had been there and done it all before and I was grateful for his help. He taught me when and what to say when needed, which, where Danny was concerned, was important.

'I saw first-hand how the players really looked up to Saint. He was a superb foil for Danny. He had the right amount of understanding and humour for every occasion. They were great days for all around the club and Saint was a big part of that.

'God bless, mate.'

Defender **Paul Bernard Jones** played over 600 games in the Football League during his career, 445 of these for Bolton Wanderers, and his last club was Stockport County.

In the words of Kevin Francis

'My time at Stockport County was made smoother when I first got there due the hospitality of John Sainty. It's never easy being the new kid at school and he recognised that and made sure my family and I were okay at every turn. This made focusing on playing easier.

'John bounced off Danny so well that there weren't any misunderstandings of what was expected. The calm to Danny's chaos, John was the voice of reason … until you messed up! He became a major part of my football progression and will always be remembered fondly. His legacy will live on.'

At 6ft 7in, **Kevin Francis** was, at the time, the tallest player in the Football League. He is best remembered for his four-year spell at Stockport County, during which he scored 117 goals in all competitions, but he also played for Derby, Birmingham, Oxford, Exeter and Hull. He was named County player of the century in 2002 and represented Saint Kitts & Nevis at full international level.

In the words of Andy Preece

'Firstly, I want to say what a top man Saint was. He knew what to say to you and when to say it. He was like a best mate that you could have a laugh and a joke with, but if you needed telling some home truths, he wouldn't hold back.

'On the few occasions that I was out of the team, he would tell me I should be playing and fill me with confidence, as he knew I needed that. I felt he really rated me as a player, which was a great feeling. I would always come back stronger as a result and he had that knack with all the squad. He was the sounding board and his role was huge but probably underestimated. He knew the game and everything he said made sense.

'John definitely had a huge input on tactics and team selection, and I think Danny Bergara used to lean on him a lot. I learned a lot about man management from John, which has helped me during my later coaching career. It still brings a smile to my face when I think about my time with him.'

Andy Preece played over 500 games as a professional at Northampton, Wrexham, Stockport, Crystal Palace, Blackpool, Bury and Carlisle. However, he enjoyed the most prolific spell of his career whilst at Edgeley Park, scoring 42 goals in 97 league games and formed a prolific striking partnership with Kevin Francis. He went on to take charge at Bury between 1999 and 2003 and has since managed several other non-league clubs. His latest appointment was as manager of Chorley in May 2022.

In the words of Tony Barras

'I'm not good with words but I would say that Saint was a good, honest, straight fella with a quick wit. He was good with me and Toddy [Lee Todd] when we arrived at Stockport at 18 and 19 years old.

'He sometimes pulled a face when Danny Bergara was "on one" with us all and he was very popular with the lads. In fact, I would say that he was one of the lads as well as being our coach, because he managed to do both. He enjoyed playing card games with us and always joined us for a few beers, win, lose or draw. RIP Saint.'

Defender **Tony Barras** joined Stockport County from Hartlepool in 1990 and made just one short of 100 Football League appearances for the club. He went on to play for seven other league clubs before signing for New Mills in the North-West Counties League in 2010, for whom he played regularly until retiring two years later at the age of 41.

In the words of Bill Williams

'Saint was a top bloke, very knowledgeable about football, with a dry sense of humour and he and Danny Bergara were a great partnership. It was great to be around him, and he was a massive part of the success Stockport County achieved in that era.

'I remember one occasion when we played away at Fulham and the night before the game we got the beers off the bus and drank them whilst playing cards! John found out when he saw that all the beer had disappeared. He came to me and said: "Make sure you win today or the manager will find out!" We won 1-0, thank goodness!'

Bill Williams played as a defender in the Football League for Manchester City, Rochdale and Stockport County, for whom he made over 250 appearances during two spells at the club between 1985 and 1994.

In the words of Sean Connelly

'John was a football man through and through. I'll always remember him coming to watch me play for Hallam FC before I went full-time with Stockport County. He'd made the trip over the Pennines and pulled me after the game and said: "Well, that was a waste of time!"

He was well respected by those who knew him for his football knowledge and dry sense of humour. Saint was a massive part of those successful days in the late 80s and early 90s who I will always remember fondly.'

Sean Connelly played under four different managers and made over 300 league appearances for Stockport County between 1992 and 2001 before subsequently moving to Wolves and Tranmere Rovers. During his time at Edgeley Park, he also qualified as a chartered physiotherapist and he eventually finished his playing career to link up again with Dave Jones, this time as physiotherapist at Cardiff City. Sean now has a similar tole with the Football Association of Wales.

In the words of Chris Beamont

'John was great company and very popular with the lads. One memory that sticks out straight away occurred during a long journey home after an away midweek night game that we had won 1-0. We were having a few drinks on the coach when the driver pulled into the services to go to the toilet.

'After the players began complaining that we had stopped, John, who always sat on the front seat of the coach, moved across to the driver's seat and started the engine. The driver saw what was happening and by the time he had dashed back to the coach, John had moved it forwards a few yards with all the lads cheering, but the driver was certainly not happy with him!'

After making 258 league appearances for Stockport, midfielder **Chris Beamont** went on to feature in Chesterfield's run to the FA Cup semi-finals in 1997.

In the words of Mark Payne

'John was a very unassuming man. You hardly heard him but always knew he was there. So, when he spoke, you listened. It was a great gift to have and I had many a conversation with him and not always about football.

'He was the perfect match together with Danny Bergara, who was more highly strung. John was a true gentleman and a very big part of County's rise. Sadly, now gone, but never to be forgotten.'

Mark Payne returned from a successful spell in Dutch football to join Stockport in 1988. The midfielder played in 87 league games for the Hatters, scoring on 16 occasions before moving on to Rochdale in 1991 in an exchange deal that took Peter Ward to Edgeley Park.

In the words of Phil Brennan

'I first met John Sainty when he was part of the coaching set-up at Stockport County with Eric Webster. At the time, the club was continually short of money and Eric always welcomed supporters to help out with voluntary work around the club.

'I would often chat with Saint over the coming years and I remember that he was worried when Danny Bergara was appointed as manager that he would be deemed surplus to requirements. He need not have been, as he went on to forge a great relationship with the Uruguayan and, alongside Dave Jones, the trio completely rejuvenated the fortunes of my football club.

'History shows that in the ten previous seasons to Bergara's appointment, County had conceded more goals than they had scored before instantly reversing that trend in every one of the following six terms.

'I always enjoyed our chats about the transformation of County from a struggling team to one that gained promotion from the basement division and reached several Wembley cup finals and, as a former striker, Saint was always pleased to talk about the way that County's forwards were at the top end of the end-of-season scoring charts.

'Even after Saint had left County and moved to Southampton, over the following years we spoke on several occasions and almost always the conversation involved Stockport County. On one such occasion, after the club had dropped into non-league football, Jim Gannon's team were struggling in the National League, having lost the three previous games. Prior to kick-off at Kingfield, the home of Woking FC, a voice behind me said: "This wouldn't have happened under Danny Bergara!" I turned to see that a smiling Saint had taken up a seat behind me and the rest of the media team.

'We had spoken only recently about the fact that I was working on my biography of Danny and, without telling me, he had driven over for a chat and to see what was happening to his beloved County first-hand. Although we had spoken several times since then, that was to be the last time I would spend time in his company and, in true Saint tradition, he made a lasting impression on me whilst talking about his personal memory to be included in my forthcoming book *The Man from Uruguay*.

'To paraphrase his own comment about Danny Bergara, I would say that I, too, have met many people in football and it was an honour to have known and worked with someone like Saint, who was so good for the game of football.

'God Bless you, my friend.'

Phil Brennan was Stockport County's press and media officer during John's time at Edgeley Park. A lifelong County supporter, he also worked as a freelance journalist and was the author of Danny Bergara's biography *The Man from Uruguay*, published in 2013.

11.
ANOTHER DOOR OPENS

THERE IS no truer saying in life and particularly in football than 'when one door closes, another opens'. After Danny's departure, Dave was placed in temporary charge until the directors offered him the manager's position from the start of the following season.

He immediately appointed me as his assistant. Dave proved to be a really good manager and was happy to leave me to do the majority of the coaching, which was exactly where I was at my happiest. We would discuss team selection before each game but ultimately the final decision was down to Dave. Mind you, Dave always used the term 'silent assassin' to describe me and the role I performed at the club! I was quite happy to have that description used about me and had gone from 'Saint' to 'silent assassin', although, fortunately in other football circles, I continued to be known as just 'Saint'.

The fans still loved Danny and made it clear they were not happy about his departure or particularly pleased about the new regime. Dave had to be pretty ruthless in his approach as he began to dismantle the team Danny had built and start to build one that we could work with in the way that we wanted. We wanted to change the way the team played and, instead of being dependent on the long-ball game Danny preferred, we set out to create a more well-rounded side that would be better equipped to deal with life in a higher division.

Dave's first season in charge, 1995/96, was nothing spectacular and County finished mid-table in the Second Division. We knew the team wasn't good enough, but it was going to take strength of character to weed out the bad apples and, with my support, Dave did just that. The transition period for us both was tricky, as we had been a group of friends, with Dave and I being the players' go-between to Danny. But perseverance paid dividends in the end. We wanted big-hearted, determined players who could make things happen and express themselves, and that is exactly how the team started to build.

Dave's ideas were also governed by money, as there was no way the club could sustain a crippling wage bill. So, an ingenious bonus scheme was worked out. The more points amassed, the money went up, which seemed the best way to reward success and we found the majority of our players committed themselves to extended contracts at the club.

Dave was in no way a disciplinarian, but he wanted to do things fairly and in the right way. He decided suits and ties would be worn for home games, but tracksuits for away games. Long-distance away matches were overnight hotel stays, leaving the ground at around 1pm and upon arrival at our destination we had an evening dinner, then off to bed. After breakfast the next morning, there would be a walk at about 11.30am, a pre-match meal at midday and then on to the ground for the game in the afternoon.

I have since often been reminded about the many times that I would fall asleep over my hotel dinner the night before a game.

The priority was to get the players into their rooms, down for the evening meal and then back to their rooms to settle down for the night. Dave and I would eat later with the backroom staff and my habit was to fall asleep over the dinner plate, not through drink I hasten to add, but it was just something I did. I could always fall asleep anywhere at the drop of a hat, but poor Dave and company would have to wake me after they had finished their meal, stand me up and point me in the direction of my room!

Whilst at Norwich, my great friend Graham Wren once accompanied me to an end-of-season managers 'do' at the Royal Lancaster Hotel in London and he never tired of reminding me that on the way back in the car I fell asleep, with my head on his lap, all the way back to Norfolk!

Dave had all the backing of chairman Brendan Elwood and the board and he wanted to bring in experienced players who, for whatever reason, were not getting games with their present clubs and we began the task of persuading them to come in and do a job for County. On our radar initially were former County striker Brett Angell, who was out of favour and training with youth-team at Sunderland, the Wolves pair of midfielder Tom Bennett and goalkeeper Paul Jones, and Notts County's former Huddersfield midfielder Chris Marsden. We were keen to get them on board and just had to sell them the idea that Stockport were really going places.

So, with a new stand completed behind the goal, a newly laid pitch and a new bonus scheme, which meant the more games won, the more the players would earn, we were on the right lines and these factors, along with the offer of long contracts, persuaded those players it was the right move for them.

At that time, the club offices were situated under the main stand at Edgeley Park and were pretty gloomy to say the least, so the idea was for Dave and myself to interview any potential players in the newer part of the ground. We wanted to show them that, although the club had a huge history going back some 100 years, we were also a forward-thinking club that was going somewhere. My role alongside Dave was to provide progressive ideas on coaching and training and to sell the club to these players, enthuse them and make them want to join us to help the promotion dream come true.

By the summer of 1996, Dave and I had got together a tremendous bunch of lads with a squad full of characters, plenty of technical ability and everyone behind them. Slowly but surely, the Bergara legacy was fading and we were bringing in our own players, new training methods and style of play.

The new training regime started with a half-hour of stretches and warm-ups, then we played short five-a-side games, concentrating on passing and movement, and making players feel confident on the ball. Dietary advice began to be introduced, with the result that both eating and drinking habits began to change. Education and moderation became the watchwords, things that I was to take forward with even greater emphasis later in my career.

Working each day with such an enthusiastic bunch of lads was rewarding, as the players took on board the new ideas. Danny was never particularly keen on having a youth policy, but this was about to change for the sake of the future of the club. Dave initially brought in former Wigan manager Dave Philpott to introduce a school of excellence, but Philpott left to take a job at Tranmere Rovers and former Burnley player Joe

Jakub joined, having previously been assistant youth coach at Preston North End.

The 1996/97 season had not got off to a great start, but the team began to come good during September, making steady progress in the league and also starting well in the Coca-Cola [League] Cup. After beating Chesterfield 4-2 on aggregate in the first round, we faced First Division Sheffield United and were somewhat fortunate to take a 2-1 lead from the first leg at Edgeley Park. Dave and I worked the players hard in training and planned as meticulously as possible ahead of the second leg at Bramall Lane. The result was spellbinding, attacking football, just as we had trained and planned for. Imagine our delight when we ran out 5-2 winners on the night to complete a 7-3 aggregate success. Alan Armstrong hit two goals, with Tom Bennett, Jim Gannon and Brett Angell also on target.

At the same time, our form in the league continued to pick up and belief around the club grew as we came towards the draw for the next round of the cup. Of course, everyone hoped for a tie against Manchester United but, instead, we were drawn away against different Premier League opposition in the shape of Blackburn Rovers, who were not enjoying a terribly good season.

One thing did have to change on this occasion and that was our strip. Our blue home kit clashed with Blackburn's blue and white halves, which also effectively ruled out our black-and-white away kit. So, for one night only, our kit suppliers, Adidas, arranged for us to play in the yellow shirts of the Romanian national team. It must have been a good omen, as the lads played their hearts out and were well-deserved winners, the only goal of the game coming when Angell connected with a perfectly placed throw-in from 'the master' Mike Flynn and wrong-footed Tim Sherwood before guiding the ball into the net.

We received some amazing plaudits in the national press the next day, but the players continued their day-to-day tasks in the same way, working hard and not allowing the success to go to their heads. In the past, we had often lost form in league games whilst performing well in cup competitions, but this time the whole experience seemed to lift the lads to perform better. They were truly believing in themselves and remained very much in the promotion picture.

The next Coca-Cola Cup adventure was a late November visit to Upton Park and a tie against Harry Redknapp's West Ham. Our previous results had by now created a great deal of media interest ahead of the tie. But Dave and I were well pleased with the way all the team were performing, so we had no plans to change anything in the build-up to the game.

Dave was good friends with former Manchester United goalkeeper Les Sealey, now the Hammers' reserve keeper, and earlier in our time at Stockport, he had attended our training sessions once a week, concentrating on giving help and advice to our keeper, Paul Jones. Les warned West Ham boss Redknapp not to think we were easy pickings. He knew what we were capable of.

West Ham had a team full of international stars, but were not having a good season, so we felt no fear. Preparation was exactly the same as in previous rounds, a night in a good hotel in London, training the next morning at Cheshunt, Spurs' training ground (how long since I had last set foot there?), then back to the hotel for a meal, afternoon nap, then tea and at toast around five o'clock and final preparations for the match.

What was different, however, was the increasing attention the team were now getting from the media. Dave was in demand to speak to the press and the TV. It was a proper taste of the attention received at a higher level, which the players took in the best way possible. They wanted success and to push harder for promotion.

The game was a sell-out, with over 1,000 County fans travelling down to support us. Although starting off brightly, we went 1-0 down when Florin Răducioiu sent the ball past Jonesy in the first half. Going in at half-time, we knew that we still had a chance, being only one goal behind, and sure enough, with a tactical switch, the game took on a different turn.

Luís Cavaco, our little Portuguese winger, turned things around when he seized on a mistake by Julian Dicks and fired the ball home. A draw was what we deserved; the lads were as one and played the way we knew they were capable of.

Going for a beer with Harry after the game, he was quick to acknowledge how well our lads played, but Dave and I guessed he still felt quietly confident for the replay at Edgeley Park. Meanwhile, we had to get through three league games, one FA Cup fixture and an Auto Windscreens Shield [Football League Trophy] tie before the big one against West Ham on 18 December.

Still, for all the media attention we were getting, we remained the underdogs. When the day arrived, the weather had not been great and the pitch was awful, but the fans were undaunted and the gate of just under 10,000 was the biggest attendance of the season so far. Our preparation remained exactly the same as for any other home game. Both Dave and I believed in keeping things as normal as possible; it had worked for us so far, so we saw no reason to change things.

When the game began, West Ham started strongly and we went a goal down, the scorer, of all people, being full-back Julian Dicks. Dave and I looked at each other, thinking 'here we go again', but what was to come turned everything around. The lads were eager to get going and try to redress the balance and they were assisted by the Hammers' Iain Dowie who, as a cross came into the West Ham penalty area, headed the ball straight into his own goal. Then, with the visitors struggling to recover from the shock and, with the rain beating down as it only can in the Manchester area, Brett Angell headed high past keeper Luděk Mikloško to put us in front.

The noise from the crowd almost lifted the roof off the stand! We had kept calm and controlled, and it had paid off. Mind you, the second half was one long 45 minutes. The lads were up for more goals and, although we were shouting at them to keep hold of the ball, they were on fire. I think I aged a few years that night!

Although Redknapp was gracious in defeat and commented that 'we had played well', Dave and I both felt that his remarks were somewhat tongue-in-cheek and we just glanced at each other and smiled.

However, we had to keep things in perspective. There were no big celebrations, as we needed to focus and get on with the league games ahead. Promotion was still the main objective and, although we had just inflicted defeat on an expensive team which had included a number of full internationals, we had to keep the lads' heads in the right place. In fact, we were receiving so much press and TV coverage, both locally and now nationally, it was important to keep everyone's feet firmly on the ground, and that included everyone from the chairman and directors down to training staff, groundsmen, office staff and ourselves, as well as the players. The players could very easily have got carried away but, being the bunch they were, they understood what was at stake and we had little or no problem keeping them grounded.

So, after a 0-0 draw at Bury, we got past the Christmas break with a 3-2 win at Wrexham on Boxing Day and followed up with a 2-0 FA Cup win at Stoke. Then we had one more league game, at home to Millwall, which we won 5 – 1, before we welcomed Southampton to Edgeley Park for our next challenge in the League Cup. In reaching the quarter-finals, we had already beaten two Premier League clubs, so why not a third?

We were riding high and had learned a lot from our previous experiences but were certainly not intending to rest on our laurels because, as management, we were only too aware that football often has a habit of smacking you on the bum!

Much as we loved all the attention being focused on the team, we were still a Second Division side and had a job to do against Graeme Souness and his Saints side, which included household names like Matthew Le Tissier, who was regarded as 'Le God' by their supporters. But our belief was strong and we prepared for the game in exactly the same way as we always had.

The day of the game, 22 January, brought another evening of 'traditional' Greater Manchester weather, with rain lashing down and almost identical conditions to those for the game against West Ham, so we knew Southampton would not enjoy the conditions. A full house at Edgeley Park produced a deafening noise but when Egil Østenstad put Saints ahead, despite us having made a good start, Dave and I wondered if this was where the run would end. Instead, the lads were about to make history repeat itself.

Brett Angell swiftly scored an equaliser and this was followed by our little dynamo, Luís Cavaco, sending a diving header into the net. The atmosphere in the stadium was electric and, as the game reached half-time, we seemed comfortably in control.

Dave's team talk centred on keeping everyone firmly focused. He was not able to speak to each individual player in 15 minutes, so my role as quiet motivator was to tell the lads to keep it going and to make sure they gave a word of encouragement to anyone they noticed was beginning to struggle.

For the first 20 to 25 minutes of the second half, the team did all we had asked of them, but tell-tale signs of fatigue were beginning to show against a far stronger side. As the minutes wound down to full time, the onslaught became relentless. An equalising goal looked inevitable and, sure enough, after 85 minutes, Østenstad went through tired legs to score his second goal of the game.

Our supporters were crestfallen and we were unable to do more from the touchline, but there was more drama to come. Le Tissier had the easiest shot at goal to knock us out but then, from nowhere, 'Flynnie', our skipper, hurled himself across the goalmouth to deflect the ball away for a corner. It was the sort of moment nobody present would ever forget. We were still breathing, just! What a night and now we had a replay to prepare for at The Dell in seven days' time.

We travelled down the day before the game and the players trained on the seafront the next morning, slept in the afternoon and woke up at 5pm for tea and toast. It was our usual pre-match routine but when the game began, our players froze. Le Tissier took full advantage and put Saints in front. In a strange way, it settled our team down and, after the interval, we played with much more confidence and pressed forward looking for an equaliser.

A great finish by Brett Angel got us level before he was substituted for Andy Mutch, who grabbed the winner. Graeme Souness was very complimentary towards us afterwards, saying that our victory was 'well-deserved'. Amazingly, we had reached the semi-final stage of one of the nation's most important cup competitions. Not bad for a team in the third tier of English football.

The other semi-finalists were all Premier League sides – Leicester City, Middlesbrough and Wimbledon – so it didn't much matter who we drew. It turned out to be Middlesbrough, with the first leg to be played at Edgeley Park. Once again, the traditional northern weather made an appearance and, with the pitch sodden, both sides struggled to impose themselves upon one another in the first half. But after the break, a bad lapse in concentration gave Boro the lead and they went on to add a controversial second goal after Mike Flynn appeared to have been fouled.

We got the perfect start in the second leg at a packed Riverside Stadium when Sean Connolly powered home his first goal for County and we came close to drawing level when Luís Cavaco drew a fine save form Mark Schwarzer. However, the game changed when Tony Dinning was harshly sent off after clashing with Fabrizio Ravanelli and Middlesbrough were content to hold on for an aggregate victory.

We had, nonetheless, done ourselves proud during the competition and the cup run seemed to help to hold everything together as we continued the pursuit of our main aim – promotion. We also had a good run in the Auto Windscreens Shield, where we reached the Northern Area Final before losing to Carlisle United. Although it was disappointing not to reach Wembley again, we had more than enough to concentrate on with 12 league games still to be played in the remaining five weeks of the season.

With so many games to play in such a short period, it was just a question of keeping things ticking over. Dave and I often couldn't train with a full complement of players because some would be carrying knocks that either required treatment or rest. But, somehow, we got through and, in the end, to clinch promotion we needed to win one of our last two fixtures, which were away at Chesterfield and Luton Town during the last week of the season. We travelled down to Saltergate on the Monday for the game against Chesterfield. Their players must have been as tired as our lads were after a long season in which they had enjoyed an amazing run in the FA Cup that took them as far as the semi-finals. Under manager John Duncan they still had an outside chance of reaching the promotion play-offs as well, so it was certain that they would still be up for the game.

It was a foul evening and, with rain having been lashing down all day, the pitch soon turned into a mudbath. A goal from Brett Angell put us in front after five minutes and, although Chesterfield bombarded us in the second half, the score remained at 1-0 as we entered the final moments of the game. We were on the point of promotion and Dave turned to ask me how much more time remained. Goodness knows what he must have thought when he saw me bent over against a wall, almost hyperventilating. I told him to go away. I just wanted the game to be over and, thankfully, soon afterwards it was.

Having recovered, I was able to join in with the players' celebrations that followed in the dressing room and, with promotion in the bag, we must have stopped at every pub on the way home! As a result, Dave and I slept downstairs in our office, or the 'Bunker' as we called it, as we were certainly not fit to drive home.

Unfortunately, we were not able to go on and take the league title, as leaders Bury won their last game against Millwall whilst we were drawing at Luton. However, I think this was only a minor detail to our supporters, who finally had something meaningful to celebrate after living in the shadow of the achievements of their two big Manchester neighbours.

Each of the four players Dave and I had initially targeted had played an essential part in what had been an enormous team effort. Brett Angell had cost £120,000 when he rejoined the club, but he proved his worth and finished the season as our leading goalscorer. Paul Jones had done a brilliant job after taking over in goal from fans' favourite Neil Edwards, and Chris Marsden had been exceptional in midfield after arriving on a free transfer.

'Mazza' and Tom Bennett had become a great pairing in the middle of the park. Sadly, Tom's career at Stockport pretty much came to an end when he suffered a broken leg in a game against Birmingham in January 1998. Although he was eventually able to recover, he found it difficult to get back into the side on a regular basis and moved to Walsall, where his career blossomed again.

Whilst recovering from his injury, Tom and our physio, Rodger Wylde, discovered a shared interest in rock music. Both learned to play the guitar and they formed a rock band called Fracture and they played regular concerts around the Manchester area for many years afterwards.

After a decade of toil in the lower reaches of the Football League, Stockport County had finally returned to the second tier of English football after a gap of 60 years. The morning after the season finale, chairman Brendan Elwood proudly came to the ground and into the office to give Dave and I each a letter with the offer of new contracts. However, in his excitement, he handed Dave's letter to me and vice-versa. Upon opening the letter, I accepted the terms straight away and offered to sign immediately, before Brendan realised his mistake and had to prise the letter from me. Shame ... I would have been quite happy to sign Dave's contract instead of mine!

That evening, the chairman arranged a cabaret night at Cottons in Knutsford for the players and their wives and girlfriends. The following day, we were all on an open-top bus tour from Edgeley Park to Stockport Town Hall. There were a few hangovers on board and the weather wasn't doing us any favours but, despite the rain, thousands of people lined the streets to cheer and wave their flags. We were ushered out on to a balcony at the town hall. Well, I say 'balcony', but it was actually just a ledge about 6in wide and it was very congested with press and some supporters there as well and it would have been very easy to fall off.

A few days later, both Dave and I were able to agree new contracts at Edgeley Park, but obviously the games Stockport played against Southampton, as well as our wins against two other Premier League sides, Blackburn and West Ham, had propelled the whole club – and Dave, in particular – into the limelight. He had particularly caught the eye of Southampton chairman Rupert Lowe but, even so, I think the call Dave received from his agent, Jonathan Barnett, while on holiday that summer came as something as a shock.

Barnett informed him of Rupert's interest in appointing Dave to succeed Graeme Souness as manager at The Dell. I was also away on holiday, in Spain, and Dave called me to let me know what was happening. In fact, he kept me in touch every step of the way in the negotiations. Dave was naturally keen to take the job at Southampton but was not prepared to just walk out on Stockport without ensuring they received compensation in return. While all this was going on, only Dave and I knew the way things were going; apart, of course, from the two chairmen.

By this time, the players were also beginning to negotiate new contracts and Jim Gannon and his wife came in to see Dave and me to ask for a rise in salary, a deal on a car and various other requests. I remember Dave sitting back in his chair and agreeing with everything that Jim was asking for. I was sat alongside Dave and began mouthing 'no' and trying to get Dave's attention as, of course, it was no longer in our hands. I never found out whether Jim eventually got his desired requests.

During his discussions with Rupert Lowe, Dave had insisted that he wanted me with him at Southampton, as we were a team and had worked together for six years. As for me, I had no wish to be a manager again and I knew Dave trusted me to work alongside him as coach and that was what he wanted. I was delighted with the prospect of working at a Premier League club and a return to living on the south coast.

In the meantime, plans we had made ahead of the new season at Stockport were put in place, including a trip to Portugal, but ultimately these would not include Dave and myself. Instead, we had a whole new group of players to get to know and a hugely challenging task ahead of us in Hampshire, but we were ready to embrace it.

I left with memories of two play-off finals and two Football League Trophy finals at Wembley to be proud of, although not coming away as winners makes it very hard to think of them in that way. But memories of getting promotion to the First Division and the decisive game at Chesterfield will stay with me forever.

In the words of Dave Jones

'I think Danny originally felt that John and I should have resigned at the same time as he left but we disagreed, as his departure was over a personal issue and not a football matter.

'John was offered the chance to take over as manager but, instead, he suggested to the chairman that I should have a go. John had been there before, seen it and done it and no longer wanted the hassle. He was more than happy to be a No.2, the buffer between myself and the players. Nothing wrong with that. He was very conscientious and tried to be tough, but he had a soft heart and I don't think he ever wanted to hurt anybody. I think he had sometimes felt uncomfortable when having to make tough calls and that may be why he felt he wasn't a good No.1.

'I think John undervalued himself as a coach, as he was very good at it – as his record shows – but he just wanted to be assistant manager and do all the organising. He was meticulous in his planning and arranged all our trips. Although he could sometimes be a bit of a joker, he took great pride in this and was very professional and every detail was attended to in military fashion. As a result, I did most of the coaching, but he became a great ally for me. Even if he didn't agree with me, he would always back me up. There was no backstabbing or anything like that. He would never show the players anything but support for me and the decisions I made. He didn't give them any excuse to misbehave.

'John was a very private person and I think that's why he used to fall asleep so easily – he didn't want to give too much away! Seriously though, you had to draw remarks out of John regarding his achievements in the past, unless he was trying to help someone.

'He would normally never argue with anybody and just remained calm. The only time I can remember him losing his cool came during an away game against Huddersfield when I had to stop him emptying a bucket of water over their manager Neil Warnock's head! In the end, I got wetter than Neil did! I had never seen John so angry as he was that day and never saw it again.

'John always liked to embrace new ideas and new products. One of the things he became fascinated by while we were at Stockport was shaving gel. He was intrigued how a little spot of gel could turn into so much foam and thought it was going to change the world. So much so, he got some for me and the other staff, and at one stage we had ten tins in the office!

'After the cup semi-final at Middlesbrough, the staff and team stayed in the North East that night and, although we lost the tie on aggregate, 2-1, we still had the party that John had arranged. We travelled back the following day and I'm thinking, "How am I going to get these lads to play again in two days' time?" Meanwhile, John was giving out more beer and pizza on the coach! I need not have worried, as 48 hours later we won 2-0 at Peterborough.

'I thought John was having a panic attack during the game at Chesterfield when we clinched promotion. "Tell me when it's over," he kept saying and he became more and more agitated until the game ended and then he couldn't stop crying. He was so pleased for everybody and I remember he told me how proud he was of me and also himself for recommending me to become manager! I think we did stop at every pub between Chesterfield and Stockport on the way back and John arranged it all. It was the best night ever.'

Our success at Stockport was a massive tribute to everyone at the club. It would have been nice to have stayed another year to see just how far the team could have gone, but I could not turn down the opportunity to manage in the Premier League. Every player in that team was probably capable of playing as an individual at the top level.'

In the words of Mike Flynn

'John Sainty was a very important part of the success we had at Stockport County during a very special period at Edgeley Park. When I first joined the club, he and Danny Bergara were already a great partnership; they had won a promotion a couple of seasons earlier and were building on that success.

'They were two very different characters, but they worked so well together; Danny the intense and passionate manager, John the calm and reasoned assistant. He was the bridge between the players and the manager but was also a great coach in his own right and he had a great sense of humour.

'When Dave Jones took over as manager, John remained in place as his assistant manager. He was the perfect fit. He knew the club and the players, and during those first few weeks of Dave's reign when results weren't going our way, he was the one that helped keep the players upbeat. He was a great influence on everyone around him.

'Of course, history shows that County went on to enjoy another promotion and several great cup runs, including reaching the semi-final of a major cup competition for the first time in the club's history. But then Jonesy and Sainty moved on to take over at Southampton, one of several Premier League teams that we had beaten during our epic League Cup campaign the previous year.

'Looking back, I know that I learned so much about man management from John and I know that I have become a much better coach because of the things he taught me during my many enjoyable years working under him.'

Defender, **Mike Flynn** spent ten years of his playing career with Stockport County. He joined the club from Preston North End for £125,000 in 1993 and went on to make 460 first-team appearances, many as captain. In 2014, Stockport afforded him a testimonial match as a reward for his long and dedicated service. Flynn donated half the money made on the night back into the club.

In the words of Paul Jones

'The first time I met Saint was when I signed for Stockport County. He was sat in the corner of Dave Jones' office and just looked at me with a cheeky smile and said: "You'll do for me."

'He was a man who sometimes didn't say at lot but when he did speak, everyone listened. I remember a game in which we were getting beat at half-time and Dave was having a go at us, effing and blinding. Saint just calmed him down and said a few words like "keep the ball and play", which we did in the second half and won the match 2-1.

'Saint was so great at keeping things in perspective but would have a go if needed. Losing him is a massive loss to football.'

Welsh international goalkeeper, **Paul Steven Jones** followed Dave and John from Stockport to Southampton in 1997 and went on to make nearly 200 Premier League appearances for the Hampshire club. He also played for Saints in the 2003 FA Cup Final defeat against Arsenal, coming on to replace the injured Antti Niemi, making history as the first goalkeeper to make a substitute appearance in an FA Cup Final. He was capped 50 times at full international level between 1997 and 2006.

In the words of John Rutter

'I first met John Sainty when I was a young player at AFC Bournemouth a long time ago. He was one of the better coaches that I had come across and certainly the best coach at the club at that time.

'Later in life, I came across him again when we were both at Stockport County. He made it his passion to coach the not-so-good players into better players. He always gave them time to think for themselves. Saint was a really good person and had a good career in the game, improving many players on and off the pitch. I would like to add my thanks to him for helping me along the way.

'My condolences and prayers go to Lindsay and John's family.'

Originally an apprentice at Wolverhampton Wanderers, **John Rutter** signed his first full contract in September 1970, but the defender did not play a league game for the club and moved to AFC Bournemouth in August 1973, where he featured in four league games. He later played around 30 league games for Exeter City in the mid-1970s before joining Stockport County, for whom he made over 400 league appearances. He later became the club's commercial manager, a post he held until June 2008.

In the words of Kevin Reeves

'During my coaching career, when I was assistant manager to Brian Flynn at Wrexham, we came up against Saint on numerous occasions when he was at Stockport with Danny and also when he was assistant to Dave. We had a great relationship with both managers and, of course, Saint. There was always an invite into each other's office after the game and a mutual respect and humour that was not always to be found at many other clubs.'

12.
MOVING TO SOUTHAMPTON

SOUTHAMPTON FOOTBALL Club was a totally different world for Dave and me.

My first recollections remain travelling down from Manchester on a Sunday and arriving at the Hilton Hotel in Chilworth, a few miles out of the city, which was to be our home for the next few months. Having checked in, we drove to the training ground at Staplewood later in the afternoon to take our first look.

Although it was a Sunday and the main gates were locked, we could see a beautifully prepared main pitch, plus three other separate training areas. We turned to each other with broad smiles; this was a brilliant set-up and worlds apart from all we had been used to.

Reality set in when we actually sat down and took stock of all that was in front of us. A lot was going to have to change. This club and this job were both big and we wanted to get things right. The basis of all Dave's teams had been senior players and he had always managed to get them to play the way he wanted. His man-management skills were good and I had every faith that he would get people in who could do the right job.

There were some pretty illustrious members of the backroom staff still in situ. Not least, former Leeds United and England full-back Terry Cooper, who had been assistant to former manager Graham Souness.

Initially, he remained as first-team coach, but the following year he became the club's chief European scout. John Mortimore, a legendary Chelsea and Queens Park Rangers player in the late 1950s and 60s who also had a spell as manager of Benfica in the 70s and 80s, was the chief scout.

On the coaching side, there were former Saints players Dennis Rofe, who was also somewhat of a legend as a player at Leyton Orient and Leicester City, and Stuart Gray, who, as well as turning out for Southampton, had previously played for Nottingham Forest and Aston Villa amongst others. In addition, Joe Jakub moved down from Stockport to take over as youth-team coach to work alongside Stewart Henderson.

At Stockport, Dave and I were one and two and that was pretty much it, but at Southampton, the set-up would be somewhat different, especially for me. Dave and I discussed at length how things would best work for all of us and the decision was taken to elevate Stuart Gray to first-team coach and for Dennis to take the reserves, with me remaining as assistant manager to Dave.

To be honest, my first reaction was disappointment, but this was quickly followed by relief, as at The Dell, the dugouts were on the halfway line and to get to the tunnel and dressing room, you had to run the gauntlet of the home supporters, so God help you if things were not going well! If you were not winning, you would get absolutely slaughtered by your own fans, so it was lovely for me not to have to go through what I termed as 'the walk of death' over and over again. Instead, I could now take a seat up in the stands to get the overall view.

Obviously, we were not going to live at the Hilton indefinitely. Dave bought a lovely house near Chilworth, while I decided to purchase an apartment in the prestigious area of Ocean Village, a development of apartments and town houses surrounding Southampton Marina. My wife, Chris, had a good job in Manchester, so she decided to continue living in our house in Stockport with my daughter Joanna, who had a groundstaff job with South African Airways at Manchester Airport, while my son Mark had a job and his own house in Hemel Hempstead.

The apartment had plenty of room for me and for the family to come down for weekends and holidays. After a while, a few of the players also moved to Ocean Village, although they had more impressive apartments!

As expected, pre-season was a time to assess the abilities of the players we had, what others we needed and an opportunity to take things at our pace. We were hopeful the team would do well over the course of the season but knew everything was not going to happen overnight. The players had said they felt lucky to stay up at the end of the previous season, as they truly felt relegation was on the cards. We knew they needed new blood around them to make the team stronger for the season ahead and, although the budget was not that large compared to many of the other Premier League clubs at the time, it was still much better than the one we had worked with at Stockport.

After a very shaky start, during which we lost seven of our first nine league games, we finished the 1997/98 season in 12th place, which seemed to us a pretty good finish to the first season of our management in the Premier League. Dave had appointed Jason Dodd as captain and brought in several new players including Carlton Palmer and David Hirst, along with young striker Kevin Davies, the last signing made by previous manager Graeme Souness. The budget had also stretched far enough to enable us to bring down Paul Jones and Lee Todd from Stockport. Todd found it difficult to break into the Saints side and only stayed for one season before moving on but Jones, who was a full Welsh international, immediately became our first-choice goalkeeper and proved to be an excellent Premier League player.

In fact, Paul was voted player of the year by the supporters and Kevin Davies was a revelation before an injury wrecked the second half of his season. Two more experienced players were added in the shape of midfielder Kevin Richardson and full-back John Beresford and the side was beginning to take shape in the way we had planned.

I think Dave and I were fully embraced into the club by all the players and staff, and for the most part the fans could see what we were beginning to achieve. One of my other roles that I really enjoyed whilst at Stockport was to go along to the supporters' club before home games, armed with the newly handed-in teamsheets, giving our supporters the team line-up and explaining which players to look out for in the opposing team.

Chairman Rupert Lowe had seen me do this when he attended County's games against Southampton in the League Cup and he asked if I would be happy to continue the pre-match ritual at The Dell. I was more than happy to agree, but soon found out one particular downside. It was fine if Matthew Le Tissier was in the team, but if he wasn't picked, I got slaughtered, as Matt was certainly 'Le God' as far as the home supporters were concerned.

He was a brilliant and skilful player, probably one of the most gifted players I have had the pleasure of working with, but, given the position we were in, we were having to battle our way out of trouble and could not afford the luxury of picking Matt to start in every game.

The first game of the season, I remember Dave was approached on arrival at the ground by some SISA (Southampton Independent Supporters' Association) members who told him if Matt was not selected to start games, they would be out to get rid of him as manager, just like they had done to previous managers.

Matt was loved and was brilliant going forward but when he lost the ball, most times he would just accept the fact and it was quite unusual for him to try and win it back. Initially, this was frustrating for us, but we realised that the players around him accepted that, with his ability, they would cover up this deficiency.

Around Christmas, he was not pulling his weight; that much was obvious, especially to all the staff, and the decision was made to rest him, apparently for the first time in four years. So, you can imagine the outcry from the fans, but we had to weather the storm; for us, it was the right call, not picking an individual for the benefit of the team.

Another one of the fans' favourite players was Franny Benali, an absolute club legend, who was made an MBE in 2020 for achievements, defying all odds and raising millions for charity. Little wonder, as I remember him as strong and determined, someone who would walk through brick walls to win the ball and the game.

Franny was also involved in something that I had never seen before or since in football and that was when he received a standing ovation from the fans for being sent off! Dave and I were not too pleased with him at the time, as we needed 11 v 11, not 10 v 11, on the pitch, but, on reflection, I did have to laugh!

However, as the season came to a close, a new and exciting opportunity was about to head my way and I was not going to turn it down.

In the words of Dave Jones

'John could have had the manager's job at Stockport, but I was glad he chose to come to Southampton with me. Our brief was to keep the club in the Premier League while building a good young side. We did that and, in the end, we also made the club a lot of money in player sales.'

In the words of Stuart Gray

'When John came to work at Southampton with Dave Jones, I was keen to tap into his extensive knowledge of football. I loved his dry sense of humour, which was always delivered with a calm, serious expression on his face.

'He was loved by everyone at the club during his time there and will be sorely missed.'

A former professional footballer himself, **Stuart Gray** has since managed Southampton, Northampton Town and Sheffield Wednesday in addition to working as caretaker manager for a number of other teams. Since 2016, he has been defensive coach at Fulham, in which time they have earned three promotions to the Premier League.

In the words of Graham Hiley

'John was a lovely man, fun to be around.

'I was working as a sports reporter at the *Southern Daily Echo* when he joined Southampton and I remember he was always a big help in terms of making me feel part of things. This was particularly evident when I accompanied the team on pre-season tours, when I would be part of the travelling group yet not part of it, if you see what I mean.

'John would always make sure I was included on the coach journeys and at mealtimes, and helped smooth things over with Dave Jones if the manager didn't like what I had written!

'He was just one of life's good guys.'

In addition to working for the *Southern Evening Echo*, **Graham Hiley** has extensive journalistic experience within the sports industry, including roles as managing editor for Southampton FC and premierleague.com. He has written several books relating to the Saints, including *Taking Le Tiss,* Matthew Le Tissier's autobiography, in 2010. He is currently an associate lecturer at Solent University, Southampton.

13.
ACADEMY DIRECTOR

THE DAY began like so many others – into work at 8am, tea and coffee shared with any other staff who were in early – but my routine was about to change dramatically after a conversation with chairman Rupert Lowe.

He explained that professional clubs were being given the opportunity to take over the grassroots of the game and away from the schoolteachers, who for years had stifled much of the progress in this particular area. We, as a profession, were now legally handed the opportunity to take boys right through from under-nines to under-19s for training and for matches against lads of similar standards.

Whilst not advertised as competitive matches and despite results not being published, he mentioned that a league format was to be put in place in a move that would revolutionise the grassroots of the game in England. Furthermore, I was invited to take on the role of academy director at Southampton Football Club and was asked to set up an academy from the remnants of the previous school of excellence.

It was a big undertaking for the club, but I accepted the challenge without hesitation. This was something I had felt passionate about since coaching youngsters back in the 1970s and, in 1982, I had gone as far as to write a paper detailing how I felt the structure of the education and football coaching of youngsters could be improved from an early age. Even then, I firmly believed that professional football clubs should become more involved in a talented youngster's development, rather than leaving it to their schoolteachers. So, in the summer of 1998, I began a role that I not only found extremely interesting, challenging and certainly varied, but one that I was immensely passionate about. As well as the football side, the role included overseeing the welfare of the boys, meetings with parents to talk through any worries or concerns they may have had, the older boys' education and attendance at college, child protection meetings and much more besides.

A significant difference between running a school of excellence, as Southampton had been, and an academy was that the former only allowed the club to sign apprentices who lived within a certain distance from the club to which they could easily travel from their home address. Even then, it soon became evident that we were not always getting the pick of the best boys within our local area, with our main rivals being Bournemouth, Portsmouth and Reading.

We also had a satellite centre established in Bath that was affiliated to Bath College and run by Rod Ruddock. This came about because a lot of our domestic catchment area consisted of sea and forest, so we had been allowed to set up this additional facility to maintain a further catchment area stretching between Weston-Super-Mare and Swindon. Among the players to eventually come through this centre was Gareth Bale.

Changing to an academy set-up, though, now meant the club was able to bring in boys from anywhere in the country or overseas. So, with this in mind, I decided to approach the chairman and ask if, instead of having another youth-team coach, maybe we could invest in a recruitment officer to oversee all scouting of boys between eight and 19 years of age.

The chairman agreed with the idea and, whilst various names were bandied about, the name Malcolm Elias kept cropping up. Malcolm came highly recommended by our education and welfare officer, Huw Jennings, who had worked with him at Oxford United, where he ran the club's school of excellence. Malcolm was at that time working for Swansea City and had been recommended to Rupert Lowe by the former chairman of the Welsh club. Prior to this, I had in my mind my good friend Graham Wren, with whom I had worked well at Norwich, for the education and welfare post, but again, Huw was brought in on recommendation.

I had no knowledge of all the connections between these names and was just pleased that Rupert had agreed to my request for the recruitment post and, being a trusting person, I was happy to be getting everything in the best place to make Southampton the best academy it could become.

So, Malcolm was duly offered the job, although this would mean some extra work for me. With around 130 youngsters in the academy, I had to put on my tracksuit for a few months and, with a lot of help and support from Stewart Henderson, we took on the coaching to replace youth-team coach Joe Jakub, who left in January 2000. With only a few months left of the season, doubling up with Stewart would not be a problem or too much extra work. To be honest, I knew I would enjoy getting back on the pitch and my body shape certainly needed a bit of a tone-up!

It was quickly apparent that very few football clubs would prosper or strengthen from local home talent alone and I knew that we had to spread our recruitment net throughout the whole of England, then further afield to Scotland, Ireland and Wales, and eventually to Europe and the rest of the world.

Triallists were sent on recommendations by agents, both at home and abroad, and, together with Ron Arthur, the academy kit man, I would frequently be journeying to airports to take or collect players. I threw myself into my new role, attending staff meetings, directors' meetings, organising the coaching staff, attending games and taking a share of the actual coaching duties.

Luckily, I found some incredible staff to support me at that time and, as well as Ron, who was a go-to man for anything, Lucy Green, my PA, was the best administrator you could wish for and helped to keep me sane and organised. Then there were Mike and Julia Upson, who took phenomenal care of all the boys and were like second parents to them.

With Julia and Mike at the helm as house parents, in September 1999 we set up a lodge for the boys to stay in rather than send them out to digs. Located close to The Dell in Hill Road, Southampton, the three-storey building could house up to 24 youngsters and it became an integral part of the success of the Southampton Academy. It offered a comfortable and welcoming homely atmosphere, which was particularly helpful when boys were experiencing living away from home for the first time and homesickness could set in as they missed their own families, friends and a familiar environment.

Ann Smallpiece cooked delicious and nutritious food while Heather Biddlscombe, another key member of the team, cleaned for us and kept the place spick and span – very important with so many untidy young men about! Another pivotal role was held by Father Andrew, who oversaw pastoral care, always providing wise counsel and guidance.

Whenever you entered the premises, there was a really good feeling about the place. It gave the boys the opportunity to bond as a group and for them to share their experiences and help each other. I know that, even today, many of them remain in contact with each other, even though they have long since gone their separate ways. One of the lads with whom I have recently been in touch, Scott Gordon, said he would go back in a heartbeat to that stage of his life.

Julia and Mike did a truly amazing job with each and every one of those boys, while Ann's food was outstanding – the staff were often found sneaking in for meals, including me! We had so many amazing coaches whilst I was in charge – Stewart Henderson, Steve Head, Steve Baker, Keith Grainger, David Coles, who was the goalkeeping coach, and many more who were a great set of role models and guided and contributed to so many wonderful players going on to bigger and better things. They, together with Ron Arthur, were always on hand to help, especially in the out-of-hours downtime when they would happily drop in to play snooker, watch telly or simply join the boys for a chat.

Over the years, I built up a good network of scouts and we were soon taking in lads not only from throughout the UK and Ireland, but from many countries further afield. For example, Chris Baird was spotted by my contact Dennis Weir, our Irish scout. Chris was one of the lads who came to live at the lodge and found being away from home tough at first, but he gradually settled down and eventually went on to become a Northern Ireland international. Along with Alan Blayney and

Scott Gordon, the three Irish lads were a terrific group, full of character despite all struggling with homesickness from time to time, so much so that I had to take a few trips back to their families to give them regular reassurance.

The target Southampton set me was to have 20 per cent of the first team coming from academy players who had completed their three-year scholarship arrangement. We had 22 scholars on the books at the time and rarely do more than three players progress through to the first-team squad each year, but I found success in the academy went in three-year cycles, with two bad years for every one good year.

Of course, the higher any team goes, the less chance a homegrown player has of appearing in the first team. Nowadays, there is even less chance for homegrown talent to break through, as clubs bring in so many foreign players who are already well established in the game.

I now feel that British players are just there to make up the numbers. The question is why? I do not have the answer, but study and in-depth research is, to my mind, the only way forward. The longer we wait, the worse it will get and it is something that needs addressing sooner rather than later.

When looking back, I am proud to say that there is quite a formidable list of boys who came through the Southampton Academy during my time in charge, with many going on to play international football and become household names; players such as Andrew Surman – who had an agent when he was aged just 11, something I had never come across before – Tyrone Mings, Leon Best, Matt Mills, Callum Chambers, Scott McDonald, Adam Lallana, Luke Shaw, James Ward-Prowse and Alex Oxlade-Chamberlain, whose dad, Mark, was one of the academy coaches. Alex joined the club as a seven-year-old and each of the others I have named also started in the academy at a young age.

On the reverse side, unfortunately not all the lads who went through the academy went on to play at the highest level, although many did make a good living and had an enjoyable career. I remained in touch with many of them, as well as a number who made successful careers away from football. Many of them enjoy brilliant family lives and if, even in some small way, the academy helped them to know there is a life outside of the game, then I am happy.

I have extremely happy memories of my time as both academy director and coach. Coaching helps to bring out the best in the players you are working with and the academy sets the path for players to progress, if not necessarily in football, then in life. Over the years, I worked with some of the best coaches in the land and we had excellent training facilities and the most fantastic group of boys, many of whom went on to become household names, and I can honestly say I feel proud of the achievements made by us all at this time.

I feel a great sense of satisfaction in a job well done.

In the words of Dave Jones

'I felt after our first full season together at Southampton that John was not entirely comfortable in his role as No.2. I'm not sure if he felt out of his depth or if he just wanted to do something else, so I suggested the academy role and John took to it immediately.

'John was always good with the youngsters and had great vision about what was going on around him. Much of what we set up together at Southampton is still going strong today.'

In the words of John's PA, Lucy Green

'It's frightening to think that I first started to work with John in 1998. I was this young 21/22-year-old obsessed with football and to work within the game was a dream for me. To be so close to the staff and players was brilliant. John just looked after me. He was so kind, generous and thoughtful but had a wicked, cheeky sense of humour!

'What always struck me about John was that he was so calm. I never ever heard him raise his voice and I definitely heard some heated arguments in my time at the training ground. He always kept calm. Even when he was telling the young players off, he would speak to them in a way that made them realise how much they had disappointed him. He just knew how to handle the young lads really well.

'I remember John going over to Northern Ireland to talk to either Alan Blayney or Chris Baird's family about them signing as scholars. When he returned, I just remember John saying that one of them lived on or near the Shankhill Road, where all the Troubles were going on, and how awful it was. I think he was really keen to get them out of there and give them every opportunity possible.

'John and Ron Arthur were the "Del and Rodney" of the football club, always getting involved in something. John always had a newspaper so he could follow the horse racing that was happening each day and I think they had a gardening business on the side at one point! Throw Bongo [football agent Gary Williams] into the mix and, well, I can only imagine what they got up to!

'Sometimes it felt like things just always happened to John and, by that, I mean that he could be quite unlucky. We had these sponsored cars that the staff would use and when John was using one it got broken into. This can happen to anyone, of course, but the thieves stole a brand-new laptop which belonged to our chief scout at the time, John Mortimore. I think Morts had only had it a day and I have no idea what John was doing with it, but it's just the sort of thing that would happen to him.

'Daphne, the chairman's secretary, reminded me recently about an occasion when she had bumped into another one of our academy players, Andrew Surman, whilst out with her daughter, but Drew thought she was Daphne's granddaughter. Daphne saw the humour in it and told John the story, but John being the wind-up merchant he was made a point of telling Drew that she was sobbing and distraught at what he had said! She wasn't, of course, but Drew was mortified, poor fella!

'Both Daphne and I were very fond of John. Some of his exploits probably didn't bear close inspection, but that was what made it so much fun working with him. We'd just laugh! They were happy times with a lot of mickey-taking at everyone's expense. When I think back to those times, it never fails to make me smile.'

In the words of Lodge House parent, Julia Upson

'My involvement with Southampton FC started in 1979, when the first apprentices came to stay with my family and, through the years, we had a succession of trialists and apprentices lodge with us, some for just a few days, others for a few years.

'In the late 1990s, a chance remark to Ron Arthur, who was dropping off a trialist to stay, changed everything. Ron mentioned that the club had acquired a large property in Hill Lane that was to become known as The Lodge and was currently run by a member of the coaching team. My words to him were: "Oh, I wish I'd known about that role, I'd have loved it."

'John, who at that time was the academy director, heard about my remark and it stuck with him, and when the role became vacant just a few months later, he approached me and my husband, Mike. During my 11 years running The Lodge, I was privileged to work with so many talented individuals, both on and off the field.

'Even after John moved on from Southampton, we remained close friends with both him and Lindsay, and even after Mike passed away, we continued to stay in touch. I will always be grateful to John for changing my life and giving me the opportunity to fulfill a lifetime ambition of working with young footballers.'

In the words of David Coles

'I first met John Sainty when he was academy director at Southampton FC. I knew he had enjoyed an extensive career in football, both playing and now in coaching. I was recommended for an interview as academy goalkeeping coach by the late Dick Bate and Steven Rutter, a former colleague of mine at Yeovil Town. Not really knowing Saint, he had called and invited me down to Southampton on a Sunday, due to the fact that the season was in full swing. As I was still playing in local league football and working as a residential social worker at a school in Berkshire, it was the best day to meet.

'On my arrival at the old Dell, I noticed this suited man walking like a penguin across the car park to the offices at the stadium. I waited a bit, as I was miles early and didn't want to seem over-keen, so to speak. After waiting for ten minutes,

I heard someone bang on my window and ask me: "Are you coming inside? It's David, isn't it? I'm John Sainty." My mum was the only one to ever call me David, so I thought I was in trouble! After getting to know John, I let him know that my mum only called me David when she was angry or mad at me, so, of course, he would then use it to useful effect at times when he thought appropriate!

'The interview went really well as I read from my diary when we entered the office and John had done quite a bit of homework on me. Introductions were exchanged before I even sat down before John asked me when I could start. I looked at him and said: "Don't you want to know what I have done or what qualifications I have for the job?" He replied: "No David, I have already spoken to lots of people who have said you would be great for this role and I am willing to listen to the recommendations and offer you the job."

'I was gobsmacked that he knew all about my playing career, where I worked and how many children I had, just like that! The complication with the job for me was that I worked early mornings at the school, was off in the afternoons, then went back to the school until ten at night. That was five days a week. On top of that, I also played semi-professional football, so when I explained to John, he just raised his eyes and suggested that if I quit playing and put my energies into coaching, who knows where it might lead to?

'John was not the only one to tell me to quit playing. Former West Ham goalkeeper Mervyn Day, who had also recommended me for the role, had told me to do the same on one of his goalkeeping schools that I often worked on in the summer. So, after Mervyn and John had both ganged up on me, I took their advice and went part-time with the academy and continued to work at the school.

'John made it clear that he would help in any way he could to help me on my coaching travels. He had organised for me to go and complete both FA 'A' licences for goalkeeping and outfield play, which were becoming extremely important for all coaches.

'The day we had an open training session at Staplewood training ground was interesting! We were short of goalkeepers in the academy at all age groups, so Saint put a notice in *The Pink*, the local Saturday evening football paper, that we were to hold open trials on a free Saturday during an international break.

'He specified an age range from eight to 16 years. Well, on that morning, we must have had 50 goalkeepers across all age groups, with me and Gerry Peyton being the only two recognised goalkeeping coaches. I said to Saint: "We can't have 25 goalkeepers in each group!" Now, this is where John was cute. Remember, only my mum called me David. He said in his calm manner: "David, I have sorted it." To which I calmly enquired: "How?" He replied: "I have Denis Rofe and Stuart Gray here, so they can take a group each with you and Gerry, so you can have 12 and a half goalkeepers each to a group."

'Seriously, these were first-team coaches who didn't have a clue on goalkeeping and admitted it there and then, but he didn't care and he gave us all a topic on goalkeeping. After 40 minutes, we switched groups so that we got a look at everyone and, you know what, it was an unbelievable success and we found one goalkeeper that actually went on to play for the first team for Southampton!

'I had been working at the academy for five months when I noticed that the first-team manager, Dave Jones, was observing training. We spoke on occasions and he asked me questions around my training methods. Then, one evening, he asked if I would like to come and work with the first-team goalkeepers as the then first-team goalkeeping coach, Gerry Peyton, was leaving for Sweden.

'I agreed to do so over the period of Easter holidays, as my schoolwork had ended for the break. I rang Saint after training to tell him, but he already knew about this and, when I asked how, he said he had orchestrated it because it was a great opportunity for me. Whilst I thanked him, he added that he knew I wouldn't have to wait long!

'There have been many people I have met who have helped me in my career, but none more so than John Sainty. He seemed to have a plan for me the moment our paths crossed and I will always be thankful for that.'

As a player, goalkeeper **David Coles** served at five different clubs whilst making over 150 appearances in the Football League. He coached at the Football Association as a goalkeeping coach before being engaged at Southampton, where he remained until 2005. After a spell as head of goalkeeping at Bristol Rovers, David once again returned to Southampton.

In the words of James Beattie

'I would like to say how sorry I was to hear that John had passed; he was a very good man. I will always remember when I signed for Southampton at 20 years old. It was the first time I had been living away from my parents in Blackburn. John seemed to always be around at Staplewood and he was one of the guys that really helped me settle in with his kind words of encouragement.

He made me feel that he was really excited that I was at the club and how bright the future could be if I worked hard and dedicated my life to football.

'John was immensely passionate about the game and about the club. He was kind and compassionate, too, and well respected by me and all the playing squad. He was quick-witted as well, being sharp to come back with any banter sent his way!

'Looking back on it now, I cannot underestimate the role he played in settling me down, always being there with words of wisdom and calmness. During my first season at the club, he remained a constant source of encouragement, despite the dire situation the team was in and in the end came elation when we avoided relegation. Everyone played their role and John certainly played his with myself and I'm sure many other members of the team.

'I will treasure his memory.'

James Beattie joined Southampton in July 1998 valued at £1m, as part of the deal that took Kevin Davies to Ewood Park for a £7m fee. Beattie's initial impact was positive, earning him the club's player of the season award as he helped the Saints stave off relegation the following year. After scoring 68 goals in 204 league appearances for Saints, he moved to Everton in 2005. The striker also played in five full international matches for England.

In the words of Neil Moss

'I had the pleasure of working with John whilst a player at Southampton in the late 90s. He was always someone I could go to for help and advice, and I have nothing but fond memories and gratitude for the time he spent with me.'

Neil Moss was 20 years old when he joined Southampton from AFC Bournemouth for £250,000 in December 1995. He made 24 league appearances for Saints before returning to Bournemouth in February 2003 and went on to make over 150 appearances for the Cherries. Since then, he has had two spells as goalkeeping coach at Bournemouth, a position which he still currently holds.

In the words of academy kit man Ron Arthur

'Most of my memories about my old friend John Sainty would be unprintable, but I can remember one incident as if it was yesterday.

'Dave Jones held a pilot's licence and invited John and Dennis Rofe to go with him for a flight in a light aircraft. I drove them down to Shoreham Airport and we met Dave, who was co-piloting the plane. When we arrived, I was told that I was going with them, so we clambered into this very small, four-passenger, two-door light aircraft. It looked more like an Airfix model!

'We flew over to Le Touquet and it was a lovely calm flight until we went to land. We bumped down on to the tarmac and the pilot flew off to try again and did another round of the airport. John did not take this very well and told Dave and the pilot if he did that again he would kill him! Anyway, after we landed safely, we spent a couple of hours in Le Touquet having a few beers before returning to the airport for the flight back.

'As we flew over the English Channel, it became dark and we hit a sea fog and couldn't see a thing. By this time, the few beers John had drunk needed to make an exit and he got out of his seat and went to put his hand on the door handle muttering that he needed a wee! Thankfully, Rofey jumped forward and stopped him before John made an exit into the Channel.

'The fog had got a lot thicker and the pilot had to find Brighton before he could follow the coast back to Shoreham. John was on the edge of his set for the rest of the flight and I

Looking on (far left) as manager John Bond encourages the City players ahead of extra time in the 1981 FA Cup Final at Wembley. (Alamy)

The Railway Inn at Woodley in its heyday. Although the building still exists it is no longer a public house. (Courtesy of Phil Brennan)

Although it was a fancy dress event, I really was doing the cooking again, this time manning the barbecue whilst our pub side took on another local hostelry. My son Mark is the angel on my right but I'm not sure who was the lifeboatman! (Author's collection)

Pre-season 1991/92 with Stockport County. Taking a moment's break during one of Danny Bergara's training camps. Danny is on the far right of the bottom row. (Courtesy of Phil Brennan)

Danny Bergara, right, pictured at our homecoming after County's defeat against Stoke City in the 1992 Autoglass Trophy Final, the club's first-ever appearance at Wembley. I learnt such a lot from Danny, and he remains a legend at Edgeley Park to this day. Darren Knowles is raising Danny's arm whilst Dave Jones, Rodger Wylde and I are in the background. (Courtesy of Phil Brennan)

Peter Ward and David Miller help one of the dray horses enjoy a pint outside Robinson's Brewery in Stockport. The company were the club's sponsors, and we are all wearing our Wembley suits prior to 1994 Play-Off Final, which we lost … again! (Courtesy of Phil Brennan)

Issuing instructions to Stockport's Darren Knowles and Brett Angel during a stoppage in play. (Author's collection)

With Dave at Edgeley Park not long after he had taken over as manager. (Courtesy of Phil Brennan)

County's squad ahead of the 1995/96 season, Dave's first full season in charge. (Courtesy of Phil Brennan)

The Saint at Saints! Dave and I flank chairman Rupert Lowe (bottom row, centre) at the photo shoot ahead of the 1997/98 season, our first with Southampton. (Author's collection)

Enjoying a cup of tea with a surprise visitor to our office at The Dell, Australian actress Emily Symons. My 'go-to man' Ron Arthur has also stepped in to join myself and Dave.
(Author's collection)

In my new role as Academy Director at Southampton and pictured with the 1997/98 Southampton youth-team squad.
(Author's collection)

With my second wife Lindsay, we married in 2005.
(Author's collection)

My daughter Joanna on her wedding day at Exbury Gardens, Hampshire in June 2007.
(Author's collection)

Putting my refereeing qualifications to good use. I am about to take charge of a Nuffield Hospital charity match at AFC Bournemouth's Vitality Stadium.
(Author's collection)

Whilst working for the Press Association I was delighted to catch up again with former Southampton striker James Beattie.
(Author's collection)

With my colleague Jay Astley (far right) and one of the local coaching directors during the Kick Worldwide coaching trip to China in 2016.
(Author's collection)

'That's my grandad!' My granddaughter, Eyvie, spots me on the legends wall outside AFC Bournemouth's Vitality Stadium, with help from my son-in-law Marc. (Author's collection)

'Braving the Shave!' In 2018 I lost my hair to raise £130 for Macmillan Cancer Support.
(Author's collection)

The best book I ever read! How lucky was I to have known and played with such a man as Dave Mackay.
(Author's collection)

All lit up for Christmas and New Year 2019/20. One of the last photographs of John taken at Kingston Lacy House, Dorset. (Author's collection)

John Sainty 'The Saint' - a man who dedicated his life to football. (Saints TV)

remember him getting off looking as white as a ghost, very quiet and making no wisecracks!'

In the words of Jason Dodd

'I remember John very well. He was a lovely fellow and so unassuming. That's the trouble with professional sport, especially football; so many people pass underneath the radar and John was never one to make a fuss. He might have received more recognition for the players he brought through the Southampton Academy, but that was the way things were.

'During my career, I underwent a big operation because something in my ankle had fused (I still have trouble with it now) and John was very sympathetic. He was just a real gentleman who didn't get the credit for all he did and now he's gone, it makes you think.'

England Under-21 international **Jason Dodd** joined Southampton from Bath City in 1988 and went on to make just shy of 400 league appearances during his 15 years with the Saints. He left to join Brighton in 2005 but, after only seven appearances, he was forced to retire through injury. He has subsequently managed at nearby Eastleigh and Gosport but returned to St Marys as academy director/chief coach in 2009. He left this position in 2014 and is currently a member of the physical education department at Winchester College.

In the words of Kevin Bond

'Saint and I lost touch after we all went our separate ways post-Manchester City, but I know he struck up a great relationship with Dave Jones, who he also assisted successfully. Latterly, I spoke with John on a few occasions after he came back south to work with the academy at Southampton. Even after long periods without contact, it seemed easy and like only yesterday when we got chatting. They were the best days, ones I remember with great fondness. John was a big part of that.'

In the words of Chris Baird

'I first came into the Southampton Academy from Northern Ireland when I was 16 years of age. As academy director, John was one of the first people I met and, with me not knowing anyone, he helped me settle in well. If I needed anything, he was always a person I could approach very easily and rely upon.

'John was always straight and honest with me from the start and, over time, we became really good friends. I'm very thankful that I met him. He was such a great person, on and off the pitch.

'I will miss him a lot but am so glad to have known him.'

Chris Baird started his playing career at Northern Irish club Ballymena United before moving to Southampton in 1998. He went on to progress through the academy and, in 2001, signed his first professional contract with the club. After making 68 league appearances for Saints, he moved to Fulham in 2007 and later enjoyed spells at Reading, Burnley, West Bromwich Albion and Derby County. Usually playing as a defender, he also gained 79 full international caps for Northern Ireland between 2003 and 2016.

In the words of former Southampton apprentice professional, Christopher Lewis

'My standout memory of John came during my last year as a schoolboy at Southampton, when I was aged 16. It was decision time regarding which boys would get apprenticeships and I was playing in a match against some trialists. I was already on

Southampton's books as a schoolboy but was nervously waiting to know if I would be signed as an apprentice.

'The game went really well for me, and I scored six goals. But John kept me grounded and said, "You know where the goal is – not a bad habit for a centre-forward," and then proceeded to list the parts of my game that I needed to work on.

'He was very caring towards all of the players and even when I was eventually released two years later, he explained the club's decision to me in a compassionate and understanding way.'

14.

THE END AT SOUTHAMPTON

WHILST I was building up the academy structure, Dave continued to do the same with the first team.

He was in the second year of a five-year plan as more new players bedded in. With Terry Cooper taking up his new role as the club's first full-time coach in Europe, Stuart Gray was promoted to take his place, whilst Dennis Rofe moved from the academy to take over from Stuart as reserve-team coach.

Although Southampton supporters were naturally disappointed to see Kevin Davies leave for Blackburn in the summer of 1998, there was certainly some consolation to be taken from the £7m transfer fee, seven times the amount the club had paid for him little over a year earlier, and the arrival in his stead of another promising young striker in James Beattie.

Beattie travelled in the opposite direction, arriving from Ewood Park, together with England international Stuart Ripley, for a third of the amount received for Davies, and his emergence during the 1998/99 season was the main bright spot in a campaign that turned out to be one long struggle against relegation.

It would be fair to say that the team's form dipped in comparison to the previous campaign and many people in the press were writing off Saints by mid-December when they were in 19th place, one point off the bottom of the table. In the end, wins in each of their last three games of the season ensured safety in 17th place. In the last of these, two priceless goals from Marians Pahars, a Latvian international who Dave had signed from Skon to Riga in February but whose debut had been delayed due to work permit issues, brought a 2-0 win over Dave's old club, Everton, to guarantee safety. The same month, Dave had also brought in another one of our former players at Stockport, Chris Marsden, who arrived from Birmingham and would go on to be a future Southampton captain, leading the side in the FA Cup Final against Arsenal in 2003.

For several years, the club had been looking for a site to build a new stadium to replace the old Dell ground which, by then, had a capacity of just over 15,000. Plans to move to a site near the village of North Stoneham near Eastleigh had recently fallen through but, at the end of the season, chairman Rupert Lowe announced the club was to move to a 32,000 all-seater stadium within walking distance of the centre of the city on the banks of the River Itchen. Construction work began shortly afterwards and the new stadium was scheduled to be ready for the start of the 2001/02 season. There was great excitement about the move and it seemed that the club was finally taking a huge step forward. But for Dave, in particular, that was soon set to change.

Having avoided relegation the previous season, Dave hoped that his long-term strategy would begin to show results in 1999/2000 but, before the season had even started, my dear friend and colleague had been the victim of accusations of the very worst kind and far removed from football.

In between his playing and managerial careers, Dave had worked in child welfare and was now accused of having abused boys in his care. A police inquiry resulted in his arrest and, although he was released, the case was far from closed. With these allegations hanging over him, Dave stated his innocence and stoically did his best to carry on with his work.

The players and staff gave him their full support but, by the turn of the year, the team found itself too close to the relegation places for comfort, although the supporters also continued to treat Dave well throughout. In January, a date was set for his trial the following November. With the date set so late in the year, it meant that not only would this affect the balance of the current season, but also the following pre-season and a large part of the next season. With this in mind, the club stepped in to place Dave on a 12-month leave of absence.

Had a temporary appointment been made from within to replace Dave, then the club's line might have been more convincing, but Glenn Hoddle had been seen shopping in Southampton just two days earlier and there was already plenty of speculation going around. Hoddle signed a 12-month contract as 'temporary' first-team manager and brought along his assistant, John Gorman, whilst Dave was going through the most turbulent time of his professional life and eventually decided to bite the bullet.

The accusations Dave and his wife, Ann, were living with had been incredibly difficult for them and for their family. But Dave handled himself throughout with incredible professionalism and fortitude and I had his back from start to finish, knowing the man as I did for so long, working alongside him, that there was never any doubt in my mind that these accusations were not true.

I was prepared to stand up in court to defend him if he needed me to, anywhere, any time and in any place.

When the case eventually came to court, 18 months after his ordeal began, it was thrown out in its first week due to a total lack of evidence and Dave was cleared of all charges. Southampton paid off the remainder of his contract and he left the club. In January 2001, Dave continued his career in management, taking charge at Wolverhampton Wanderers.

Thankfully for me, having been given the academy director role, I was set to stay. Had I still been Dave's assistant, I imagine I would have closely followed him through the door. As far as the academy was concerned, Glenn and John had enough on their plate and were more than happy for me to get on with the set-up that was beginning to take shape. They had no issues with anything to do with the academy.

The 1999/2000 season saw us enjoy a run to the semi-finals of the most prestigious competition for under-18s in youth football, the FA Youth Cup. Stewart Henderson and I always had a good feeling about that season's group of youngsters. In addition to a decent set of second-years, we had a number of first-years who were capable of stepping up when required. We didn't have any big stars amongst our ranks, but the team showed great commitment to weave their way through some very difficult early rounds at Reading, Bolton and Crewe to reach the last four.

That's not to say our squad did not contain individual ability, but their best asset was their unity and collective spirit. Our goalkeeper, Alan Blayney, had left the academy at the start of the season because he was homesick for Northern Ireland, but he continued to fly back for games in the FA Youth Cup and it rekindled his appetite for the game, and he eventually resumed his scholarship.

The skipper, Matt Davies, was an England under-16 international, as was Brian Howard, and we had Australian prospect Scott MacDonald up front and another Aussie, Mark Graham, at the back. Chris Baird would go on to win full international caps for Northern Ireland and Adam Wallace provided plenty of pace going forward, but there was a lot of chopping and changing going on in the side as we struggled with injuries at times. Mind you, there were plenty of players just waiting for a chance to come in and try to hold down a place.

Our semi-final opponents over two legs were Coventry City, who were runners-up the previous season. We made a tentative start to the first encounter at Highfield Road and Coventry came at us hard before we gradually imposed ourselves on the game. After falling behind in the second half, Wallace grabbed an equaliser and we were unfortunate to have a goal disallowed for offside in injury time.

The club had never reached the final of this competition but, with the second leg to come at The Dell in front of over 4,000 supporters, we obviously fancied our chances of becoming the first group to make it, although, despite having home advantage, there was nothing much between the two sides. But we were caught cold this time as Coventry came at us like an express train. They were ahead within three minutes and we could easily have slipped further behind. Once we had settled, we produced some better football and there was no shortage of commitment, but we had met our match in a very useful Coventry side. Their goals across the two legs were both scored by Gary McSheffrey, the youngest player ever to have appeared for the Sky Blues in the Premier League.

It had very much been a team effort off the pitch, too, with Steve Head acting as Stewart's assistant on matchdays, the physio, Phil Wilson, doing his best to get everyone fit, Andy Spink working on nutrition and, of course Ron Arthur, our kit man, ensuring everything was in place.

Returning to first-team matters, Glenn and John were only in post for just over a year and resigned at the end of March 2001, with Stuart Gray stepping in as interim manager from March until October. A 15th-place finish in the Premier League at the end of the 1999/2000 season was then followed by a mid-table finish the following year – the club's last season playing at The Dell.

Stuart was appointed on a permanent basis in the summer and I was pleased for him. We had always worked well together, although it was during this time, in May 2001, that the bombshell fell. Things were going really well, or so I thought. Everything that I had planned for the academy had fallen into place. Scouting, recruitment, coaching. The Lodge was a very happy and contented set-up, everyone was working well together – a complete team with a good squad of young and talented players. However, behind the scenes, something, of which I never got to the bottom of, was sending me down a slippery slope and ended in my removal from the role of academy director.

I still knew how to spot talent when I saw it and knew it was something instinctive in me, so I was going to carry on and give the role my best shot. Many years later, I discovered some of my diaries from that time. I was working incredibly long hours, travelling both home and abroad and was very often in my office between 6am and 6.30am in the morning. I was not seen by anyone at that time, although my work ethic was never in question, but things were about to change once again and not in a particularly good way for me. It seemed that Huw Jennings was set to replace me as academy director, with Malcolm Elias alongside him.

Maybe I am too trusting but again I had not seen this coming. Never one to make a fuss, I was offered the job of chief scout to take over from John Mortimore, who was about to retire. Some might have seen that as a step upwards. I could never be sure, but I accepted the role. Better to have a job than not to have one at all. So, much more travelling would be on the cards.

However, it didn't end there as, in October, Stuart Gray was dismissed and Gordon Strachan was appointed manager. At first, he seemed to leave me to get on with things and I had little or no verbal contact with him. I found this strange, as managers would normally often liaise with their chief scouts to get reports on any possible future signings or players of interest. Again, all was eventually revealed and yet again, out of the blue, a certain Ray Clarke, whom I had coached at Spurs as a schoolboy, turned up.

I had not seen this coming either. Believe me, it was with complete surprise that Ray turned up at the training ground one day and introduced himself as my assistant. I was more than happy to show him around and shared various player reports with him, introduced him to our procedures and so on. Never did it dawn on me that he was actually here to sideline me, although with hindsight I should have read the script. Ray was a buddy of Gordon Strachan and had worked with him in the past.

Nothing happened for a while, but eventually I had a phone call from Daphne, Rupert Lowe's secretary, to say that he wanted to meet with me in three weeks' time. What was that all about? Nothing more was said and I continued coming in to work each day, getting in at 9am and leaving at 3pm. There was no contact from Gordon or Ray Clarke during those three weeks and nothing much in the way of work. Somehow, the writing was on the wall and, in the pit of my stomach, the feelings were far from good.

At the end of those three weeks, which seemed like a lifetime, I was summoned to the appointment with the chairman and even more surprise followed. On arriving, I found he was not there – there was only Daphne, who was given the task of informing me that my position as chief scout was to be terminated forthwith.

My face no longer fitted and all my hard work was as nothing. I felt sick to my stomach and, although it didn't really come as a shock, it hurt like hell. Perhaps, with hindsight, I should have requested a face-to-face meeting with the chairman. He obviously did not want to see me in person, but to me it seemed a fait accompli and he had bowed to a decision made by Gordon. My view has always been that Rupert Lowe was more a businessman than a football person and he took more of his opinions and decisions from those around him with football knowledge. On one hand, this was a good quality, but there were times when, regarding poor decisions, he would not veto them or stand his ground.

I had always felt I had a good relationship with him but, when push came to shove, I was obviously wrong. Again, I think I have said before, in football it is not always what you know but who you know. So, on 4 September 2003, I signed a compromise agreement to terminate my employment at Southampton.

In the words of Dave Jones

'I know John was quite upset over the way Southampton treated me. He stood by me throughout and, when my court case was over and I was acquitted in November 2000, he arranged a party at a local Italian restaurant and even got his daughter, Joanna, to sing for me.

'Unfortunately, John was not Glenn Hoddle's kind of guy and vice versa.

'On a lighter note, I remember when the club had found the site for its new stadium, Rupert Lowe, John and I were invited to attend a question-and-answer session with local residents to discuss the impact the stadium might have upon the neighbourhood. The site was in an area of the city where there was a considerable Asian population and when we were asked about what name the new stadium would take, Mr Lowe did not respond. So, I piped up and said: "What about calling it New Delli?!" John and I cracked up, but our chairman was not amused and the person who was running the meeting turned to John and said: "You've sat there all evening without saying anything. What have you got to say?" With that, John simply replied: "I would like to say two words – good night!" And, with that, he got up and walked out!'

In the words of Lucy Green

'There was a tricky period when John's role changed and he moved from academy director to the scouting side. It was just all a bit awkward, if I'm honest, but it said everything about John's character that the club wanted to make sure they kept him. Let's face it, though, what John didn't know about players wasn't worth knowing.'

In the words of Dennis Rofe

'When John arrived at Southampton FC with Dave Jones, he quickly gained the trust of the players and staff, and we had a good few years together.

'Then, when Dave was leaving to take over at Wolverhampton Wanderers, he, John and I were having a meal in a restaurant one evening and, naturally, Dave was talking about his new club. He turned to John and said that had to get a coach to join him at Molineux.

'Instead of thinking of himself, as others would have done, John said: "Well, I think he is sitting in front of you Dave." And I then realised that John was looking at me. Dave asked me if I would like to join him, but I decided to stay at Southampton. That was typical of John; instead of thinking of himself, he always thought what would be best for Dave.

'This was the John I had come to know over the years at Southampton, he was liked by all the players and staff and was a man who was loyal to his manager and would always put others first when necessary.'

Dennis Rofe enjoyed a lengthy playing career as a full-back with Leyton Orient, Leicester City, Chelsea and Southampton. After clocking up over 500 Football League appearances, he went on to have several coaching spells at Southampton as well as others at Stoke City, Fulham, Kingstonian and AFC Bournemouth. He also managed Bristol Rovers between 1991 and 1992.

In the words of Scott Gordon

'My memories of John Sainty are nothing but fondness. I can recall when he came in to become academy director alongside assistant director Stewart Henderson. We had parted company with our then head coach Joe Jakub, and John, Stewart and new head coach Steve Head were the main men during our FA Youth Cup run.

'My earliest memory of John is training with the youth-team at a really out-of-date indoor gym hall underneath the main stand at The Dell. It resembled a primary school assembly hall. This grey-haired man was taking us and all the other guys seemed to know him and kept calling him 'The Saint'. I thought that was pretty cool that he had a nickname the same as the club and it was not until a few weeks later I actually realised it was his surname!

'I always had a healthy fear and respect for John. He commanded it with his presence, but in a non-arrogant way. He spoke with kindness but also we knew not to mess with him. I cannot recall any incidents where one of the guys spoke out of line or had a bad word to say about John.

'When I think back over my time with Southampton, John will always bring back fond memories. Now, as a coach myself, I hope that I show the same kindness to my players that John showed to me all those years ago.'

Midfielder **Scott Gordon** joined the Southampton Academy in 1995 when he was 13 years of age. In 2000, he featured in the team that reached the semi-finals of the FA Youth Cup. He also came to the attention of the Northern Ireland set-up before moving on the following year.

In the words of Ian Carnaby

'When John switched to academy director, he nurtured much of the outstanding talent at Southampton – lads like Nathan Dyer, Martin Crainie and Andrew Surman – and smoothed over various problems. When he moved from the academy to become chief scout, he once again did an outstanding job.

"Ironically, he would tell me with a wry smile that the No.1 rule in football was to watch your back. Saints explained his departure as a cost-cutting exercise. John was never one to be bitter, he simply took it on the chin, but everyone knew how upset he was.'

A full-time sports journalist and broadcaster, **Ian Carnaby** is also a die-hard Southampton supporter. A frequent contributor to the club's match programme, he also writes for the *Sporting Life* and the *Racing Post*.

15
ON MY TRAVELS

AT THE start of this book, I mentioned the astonishment of a boy from Poplar travelling all over the world. Well, I certainly did do quite a bit of travelling over the years, although, as I may have also previously mentioned, I didn't always appreciate the time I spent in the countries I visited and only looking back afterwards did I begin to realise how fortunate I had been.

The Netherlands was, of course, my first trip abroad and, following on from there, I have been on pre-season visits to Seattle, Vancouver, Jamaica and Sweden, as well as a trip to China with Norwich City.

As a club, Norwich loved their overseas tours; whether it be in pre-season or post-season, there would usually be at least one trip every year. In 1980, the club decided to proceed with a summer tour of China. We flew out at the end of the domestic season in May to play four matches. Kevin Bond was our captain on tour, as Martin Peters had been allowed to pull out, whilst John Benson, who was youth-team coach at the time, had to put his boots on again and played in every game.

We began with a 2-0 win against a China National XI in Beijing, which was played in front of a crowd of around 80,000. Our next stop was in Hebei, where we defeated Hebei province by the same margin before we moved on to Peking. Here, our opponents according to the match programme were 'Ba Yi', which represented the numbers eight and one, referring to 1 August, the date of the founding of the People's Liberation Army in 1927. They were a prominent team in China at the time and the game attracted a crowd of around 60,000 people, although the match ended in a goalless draw.

End-of-season tours were always a bit tricky if you were the one trying to maintain some sort of discipline amongst players who were ready to go on their holidays. The players were told not to leave the hotel without permission but, whilst in Peking, Peter Mendham and Justin Fashanu went missing and I was sent out to try and find them.

Peter had bright red hair at the time and, of course, Justin was a person of colour, so surely there were not too many others like them to be found in the Chinese capital. Eventually, I saw a crowd of people gathered in one of Peking's many squares and my stomach dropped. But, as I got closer, I could see what had drawn their attention. There were the two players giving an impromptu display of their ball skills to the fascination of the local people!

The tour lasted just over two weeks and our final match was against Bulova Watch Company. We signed off with a 2-1 success to complete the tour undefeated. But the tour did not go completely without a hitch, with a Peking newspaper reporting that about 50 Chinese supporters were arrested during City's matches for 'whistling, cursing the referee, setting off fireworks, and releasing flocks of homing pigeons at the match'. Some of those supporters were freed after 'education', but others were either fined or detained for up to ten days.

For me, the highlights of our trip were a visit to the Great Wall and to be at the front of the queue to walk past the body of Chairman Mao Zedong at the mausoleum in Tiananmen Square. Whilst in Beijing, we also spent an enjoyable evening at the British Embassy.

As academy director and chief scout at Southampton, I travelled to Perth in Australia twice and also to New Zealand. Good memories from there, particularly buzzing around in football agent Gary 'Bongo' Williams' small Triumph sports car. It was bright red in colour and looked just like Noddy's car in the children's story books! Gary loved this car so much that he had it shipped back to the UK.

We also spotted a bigger prize in the shape of young striker Scott McDonald, who came over to play not only for Southampton, but also Celtic and Motherwell and was good enough to be capped 26 times by Australia.

A couple of trips to Rome along with football agent/solicitor Richard Glass also come to mind. Richard introduced me to Dodo, an Italian agent who whizzed me around at typical Italian speed. After he had given me a special, personalised visit to the Coliseum and the Vatican, we then stood in a field just outside the city taking in a couple of matches surrounded by big, burly Italian men in dark overcoats and sunglasses reminiscent of the mafia!

In France, I made memorable visits to Lyon and Lille, particularly a game in Lyon where I was accommodated in the VIP section. At half-time, large silver platters were passed along the row of seats with canapes, followed shortly by a tray of petit fours. Extraordinary and somewhat different to a meat pie or hot dog!

Another outstanding trip during my time at Southampton was to Lesvos, via Athens. A scout on the island, Leon Theologou, contacted the club, as he thought there may be one or two players of interest, so off I went. I remember the weather being very cold and staying in a lovely little house which was approached by going across a field track where a shepherd used to walk his goats each day, the bells around the animals' necks tinkling as they went.

Leon and his English wife, Lisa, ran a bar in Petra and she had recently had a baby and I was invited to the christening. Just like in the film *Mama Mia*, the church was on the top of a rock with many steps to get to the top. It was a very beautiful Greek ceremony, with the priest in full regalia, but what struck me as amusing was the way the congregation would wander in and out during the service to have a smoke!

The main man in Petra was the police inspector and, ironically, it was his son that was one of the players of particular interest. I was incredibly well looked after on this trip, as well as on my Italian ones.

When Stuart Gray took over as caretaker manager at Southampton, he and I travelled to Argentina and Chile, which was another incredible trip. Whilst we were out there, our hosts found out about my coaching manual and, upon my return to the UK, it was translated into Spanish by a friend called Marlet from Chile, who then sent a copy back there for them to use.

Both personally and professionally, 2001 proved to be quite a year for me. In addition to flying with Stuart to Chile in February and Argentina in October, I managed a trip to Ireland with Bongo in July, and September saw me take in a game between Rosenborg and Porto in Oslo. Here, I was looked after by a football agent named Vitor and we met up with an old adversary of mine, Graham Carr. Graham is the father of the comedian Alan Carr but had been a member of the Northampton side that made its way from the Fourth Division to the First Division in record time during the 1960s, before dropping back down almost as quickly. A no-nonsense defender, Graham and I had shared a few battles on the pitch.

Soon after I returned from Oslo, I was on my way back to Norway to watch Stavanger play Kilmarnock in the UEFA Cup before joining Stuart on the trip to Argentina the following month. My next stop was Edinburgh and, together with David Coles and another football agent, Richard Glass, we took in a game between Hearts and Dundee.

During this time, my mum was taken very poorly with heart problems and was admitted to hospital. After a very worrying time, she eventually underwent a heart operation in November from which she fortunately recovered pretty well. The same year also saw Christine and I separate and eventually divorce. We had been living separate lives, which is never easy for either party. So many changes had taken place and, as a result, we had sadly drifted apart.

There were many more trips, of course, both in the UK and in Europe, but the ones I have mentioned stand out along with many family holidays abroad to Spain, Tenerife and Florida particularly.

An amusing memory from one of Southampton's pre-season trips to Portugal occurred when we were staying in beautiful Cascais. The staff always got together in the evenings for dinner and to relax and chat about the day and swap stories. One evening, the chairman, Rupert Lowe, was sat alongside Terry

Cooper, Dave and myself and the subject turned to things we did as kids. I recalled climbing over the back of our house, going into the allotments and picking up potatoes and probably a lot more besides. Dave said he was a paper boy. I don't remember what Terry said, but he and I had a similar dry sense of humour and then the chairman said: 'I used to pick up potatoes too … in my tractor!' None of us dared look at each other. How the other half lived!

Much later on, in 2016, I was working as a passenger assistant to vulnerable youngsters travelling to school when, quite out of the blue, I was invited to go up to Stockport County to give a pre-match address to supporters as part of their series of 'Legends' talks. Of course, I was more than pleased to be invited and it was great to meet up with many supporters and staff once more.

At the meal, I also met up with Steve Bellis who, at that time, ran a company called Kick Worldwide, which sent football coaches out to China, India and Oman. Steve had a long association with County in various capacities and wondered if I would be interested in travelling to China, as he was recruiting coaches. I thought the opportunity was too good to miss, so, a few days after celebrating my 70th birthday with a party at Christchurch Harbour Hotel, I set off to China for a second time.

After catching the coach at Ringwood up to Heathrow Airport and waving goodbye to Lindsay, the initial plan was to do a three-month stint. Arriving at Heathrow, I met up with another lad called Jay Astley and we were to travel together, flying first to Amsterdam, then on to Beijing for a one-night stay before an internal flight to Canton-Baiyan, which took three hours, before finally arriving at our destination, Gaoming, after a two-hour car ride. The journey was quite exhausting, but we were duly welcomed and housed with a local family, Mr and Mrs Seng, together with their young baby.

Mr and Mrs Seng were so welcoming, taking us into their home and looking after us, but, to be honest, it seemed a huge ask, particularly as the baby was quite poorly at the time and needed medical treatment from their doctor. Unfortunately for me, I also picked up some sort of chest infection, most likely from the flight, and needed to be seen by the doctor myself. It was fortunate that we were with the Sengs and that they could arrange a couple of appointments for me.

However, despite the doctor's best efforts, I didn't feel particularly well throughout the time I was in China and I have to admit that, as result, I struggled a bit to keep pace with our schedule. We were going into schools and giving talks about football, before taking the children out into their playgrounds for kickabouts. Sometimes, with as many as 30 or 40 children, it was a bit of a hotchpotch and not quite the football training I was expecting to give.

Eventually, Jay, Will, our interpreter and I decided to rent a house and live independently, though Jay was soon whisked up to Northern China to work on a new project of football coaching. I have to admit that, although Will was perfectly decent as a person, when it came to the football coaching side he seemed in a world of his own!

For example, the scenario would be as follows. From my notes, I would decide in advance how the next day's coaching would pan out. I would plan the session and the other two or three Chinese coaches working alongside us would take a group of boys each. I would monitor both boys and coaches over each session and suggest any improvements needed along the way.

Unfortunately, this line of thought stopped when it reached Will, who, instead of using my suggestions for the next session, would instead go straight on to the internet and look up 'football coaching sessions', choose one and print off the information he found. Whilst these details were perfectly fine, from that moment on my process of putting together the session stopped. Will had the idea to conduct the session by following his online instructions word-for-word, which had never been my way.

For me, my lifelong experience of coaching has meant learning, teaching and then practising and working on strengthening individual abilities. From my point of view, a website session will not give any of the above and the pupils will not be any better or wiser about their own individual ability at the end of either that day or that week's session.

Initially, the plan was to be in China for a total of three years with a couple of trips home, but after three months I had had enough. My health hadn't been the best and the trip wasn't all I had hoped it would be. However, I don't feel the journey was a complete waste of time, as you never stop learning from both good and bad experiences. You never know what to expect, so, always best to take time to stop, see, look and listen.

Maybe I would have enjoyed my time there more had I been a bit younger and, on getting home, I vowed that I would never go back. On reflection, though, it was an experience not to be missed.

In the words of Steve Bellis

'It gave me great pleasure to take John to China in his later years to share his experience with hundreds of young aspiring Chinese children. The kids loved him and he loved being out on the grass (what there was of it), but he was less keen on the food. Turtle stir fry and fish lip soup didn't seem to do it for Saint! Thank God for Pot Noodles and McDonald's!

'Saint made a good team with his sidekick Jay Astley, who did the physical stuff on his behalf. The fact that Saint was prepared to travel halfway around the world at his age to deliver coaching sessions tells you everything about his passion for football.'

In the words of Graham Wren

'In 2008, I was invited to travel to Minneapolis to coach an under-16 girls' team at a club called Eden Prairie. John came with me and for two weeks we coached this team. They had not won a fixture, had only scored one goal all season and were totally disorganised.

'Together, we worked with the girls and won an international tournament the day before we left. They loved him and realised what an outstanding coach he was and what a brilliant experience they had received in that fortnight.

'We worked them hard but fairly and they got their due reward. It was John and I working in tandem, reaping the benefits of a 35-year friendship and when John left the game of football, I continued, using the knowledge and experience that he had instilled into my character during this time.'

16.

A WORLD AWAY FROM FOOTBALL

AFTER LEAVING Southampton, I still felt I had something to offer the game of football and I wrote to all the Premier and Football League clubs, plus eight in Scotland and four in the Republic of Ireland.

I got four interviews as a result but no offers of a job. I also received a nice reply from Neil Warnock. He couldn't help me either, but offered me tickets any time I wanted to see a Sheffield United match, which was kind of him.

So, apart from a limited time away from football between spells at Chester and Stockport, for the first time in 42 years I had to look for a job away from full-time football. I still had part-time work as a scout for Aston Villa, working for Sean Kimberley, their youth development officer, and really enjoyed the way they worked and my time with them. I was also employed by the Premier League as a matchday monitor at both under-16 and under-19 levels on Saturdays and on Sundays monitoring the under-9 to under-16 age group, as well as supplying match information for the Press Association, so my weekends were always busy.

Before my travels to China, I ran some soccer schools and also did a bit of coaching with non-league teams including

Lymington & New Milton and Bemerton Heath Harlequins. I stayed at Bemerton as co-manager with Steve Slade during the 2004/05 season, but I think you have to be a special person to work in the non-league environment, with a different mindset, working with players once a week in training. Never knowing whether they were going to be available for either the next training session or game was a constant frustration to me, having been used to working with full-time professionals. I did give it a good go but, truly, it wasn't for me. Bemerton had the worst colours I had ever seen in my life, black and white checks, but we went quite a long way in the FA Cup before a 7-0 thumping by Worcester City. I got the push in the end; I tell you, committee members know even less about football than the average director!

So many changes had taken place, but life was to change for me again upon meeting and marrying Lindsay in December 2005. We moved to Verwood and, luckily, I fell on my feet, as Lindsay was working as a receptionist at a private wing attached to the Royal Bournemouth Hospital known as The Derwent and she knew there was a vacancy for a hospital porter. My face seemed to fit and, after a chat with the matron and the theatre manager, the job was mine.

The wing had recently been taken over by the Nuffield Hospital, whose main building was on the opposite side of the town, so there were routine runs four times a day by van to take equipment and supplies between the two locations. I was part of a group of four people who conducted these runs and sometimes we would take other staff to and fro as well. In the office next door to us was Paul Markham. He was in charge of the hospital's supplies department and we shared a lot of friendly banter together. At the start there was Don, Dominic and Eddie and it was enjoyable to work as part of a team once again. When Don retired and Dom left, Eddie and I were joined by an ex-fireman, Ken, and an ex-policeman, Dave, to form a second gang of four. Eddie's son was starting off as a goalkeeper, so I was consistently quizzed about the right way forward for him. He eventually joined the goalkeeping school run by Keith Grainger, one of the Southampton coaches and I think also went for coaching with AFC Bournemouth's Neil Moss, who had been with me at Southampton as well.

Strange how often things turn almost a full circle. In 2009, whilst I was working at the Nuffield, the chance came to play in their football team against a team of consultants from the Royal Bournemouth Hospital. I was, of course, keen to play in some ways, but reluctant in others. I knew that, after two replacement procedures, my knee was not the best and my running days were well and truly over. Mind you, even in my heyday, I never ran around more than was absolutely necessary!

The charity game was duly arranged and guess where my final appearance on a football pitch was to be? Amazingly, it was at Dean Court, as often AFC Bournemouth let the pitch out for charity events once the Cherries' season had been completed. The old ground that I used to play in back in the 70s had been demolished in 2002, so this meant I was set to become one of the lucky people to have played in both the old and the new stadiums at Dean Court, and almost certainly the only one to do so 24 years apart. Even Ted MacDougall didn't manage that!

Come the day of the game, it was decided that I would play only if any of the rest of the team ran out of puff, which was fine by me. In the meantime, I would just manage the team and pass on instructions. Four teams actually took part on the day and the Nuffield team were playing for the charities Julia's House and Friends of Blandford Community Hospital. Our opponents were Hospital Metalcraft Ltd and we were delighted to come out 4-1 victors, raising £500 for the charities. I actually made a fleeting appearance, lasting about 15 minutes, during and after which I knew for sure that my playing days were definitely over!

During my time at the Derwent, a strange coincidence occurred. George, the theatre cleaner, had an extended leave of absence due to illness and the head housekeeper, Sheila, asked around for someone to fill in. I was more than happy to do the job, having always been happy to take on anything. The coincidence was that Sheila and her husband, Vic, both Bristolians, were best friends with Bobby Williams, my old mate from my Reading days, who lodged with me on his move from Bristol with his wife, Brenda. You really couldn't make it up.

I enjoyed working at the Derwent, but sadly things came to an end there when the unit was mothballed and all the staff moved over to the Nuffield at Lansdowne Road in Bournemouth. However, an opportunity came my way to move into a very different role there and I became medical records officer.

At first, I found this a challenging and interesting role, but, as in many areas of life, the people in charge changed and the working atmosphere and the full-on pressure of the role, with a good deal of computer work, made me totally stressed. Now, looking back, I believe it may have been the start of my dementia and I was also suffering quite badly with arthritic problems in my hands and fingers, the result of pulling out files from large sliding cabinets. I had to get away. Sadly, there were one or two personality clashes, although the majority of staff were amazing and thoroughly enjoyable to work alongside.

Whilst I still had my job at the hospital, I worked for a long time for the Press Association as a matchday analyst and, in my last proper link with professional football, I returned to AFC Bournemouth scouting for up-and-coming young football talent while working for Carl Robson in the club's academy; a really nice guy who, I think, respected my judgment.

Gradually, as time goes on, your contacts fade away, certainly as far as today's game of football goes. I continued to apply for jobs as they came up, but often heard nothing back, not even an acknowledgement, which can be quite soul-destroying, as I have always felt I had such a wealth of experience to offer, gained over so many years. I certainly didn't see myself as a threat to anyone else's job, but I guess all good things come to an end and I was fortunate to have had a career in football spanning almost 60 years, which is amazing in itself.

I began to wonder what my next job could be. I certainly wanted to do something, having never been one to sit around and twiddle my thumbs. Eventually, I interviewed successfully for a role as a passenger assistant for Dorset County Council. This involved working during school term only and my role was to accompany a child with special needs to school in a taxi. Each morning, I was collected from home and driven to the child's home, basically to chaperone them on the way to school and back again in the afternoon. I managed this job for the next four years before finally finishing in 2020.

In the words of Nuffield Hospital supplies manager Paul Markham

'Well, where do I begin with my old mate Sainty? We shared some great times in and out of work. I could sit for hours – and did – listening to all his stories from his football days to pub landlord.

'Sainty and I worked together in the hospital for a number of years and one recollection that I always remember was when we desperately tried to find a way of watching some horse racing. We particularly liked the Cheltenham Gold Cup meeting, so, while at work, we would walk around trying to find a screen, any screen, to watch the race. Sainty always came up trumps and would then give me the "look" as if to say "I've found a screen!"

'The lovely thing about Sainty was his generosity. He did so much for me and took me under his wing when I was new to the workplace. He would literally give you the shirt off his back and ask for nothing in return. That's a rare quality and I will always be thankful for having him in my life.

'I still miss him dearly and often think of him with a smile on my face.'

In the words of Nuffield Hospital pharmacy and medical records manager Simon Mercer

'I will always remember John as being the loveable, kind and gentle man that he was. There are few staff that come in to work every day with an infectious laugh, a roaring sense of humour and an air of slight naughtiness, which only meant you loved him and appreciated him more.

'Trying to find John in the place where he should have been often became something of a military exercise, which required one to have more stealth than he did. I often failed. Sometimes I'd find him in a room with the television on and he'd just smile, nod and then get back to work. All that said, I wouldn't have wanted him any other way. He was hard-working, had an enormous heart and always had a listening ear.

'To know he has gone from us is sad, but his personality and heart will live with me fondly until one day we shall meet again in the Nuffield Sky!'

17.
THE IMPACT OF INJURIES

INJURIES HAVE always been part and parcel of playing the game of football, both in training and in matches. Many ex-players, when they sit down and reflect upon their playing career and consider the injuries that they sustained, are surprised at the number involved. For my part, these are the ones I remember suffering. Here goes …

Forehead: A few times during my career I sustained cuts which were bandaged at the time but, like most other players, I carried on playing and was stitched up afterwards.

Chin: I remember, when standing behind an opponent who then decides to flick the ball on, getting caught on the chin as he followed through, which again resulted in stitches.

Upper body: Regular bruises, again usually as a result of players following through once they have played the ball, but, sometimes, following through without playing the ball.

Legs, knees and ankles: Always prime targets for injury in my case. Having started playing at a competitive level at a fairly young age and because of my size, I blended in with older age groups and I think my knee problems began quite early on. As I was very right-footed and mainly used my left leg simply to stand on, most tackles by the opposition were directed on to my left leg. I have had to have many arthroscopies to clean out my left knee and eventually there was no alternative but to have my first knee replacement whilst I was at Stockport. This procedure lasted pretty well, although I did not manage to get back a full bend on the knee and, whilst at Southampton, I had manipulation under anaesthetic to try and improve this. Unfortunately, it did not make much difference and I subsequently underwent a second knee replacement.

During my retirement years, I was invited by the Professional Footballers' Association to take part in a former players' study, run by the Drake Foundation, into the risks to cognitive and general health. I was delighted to say yes, as I feel strongly that research done into all these conditions will prove invaluable, provided the results are acted on.

The first part took place at my own home in September 2019 and was based upon an assessment, history of my career, my lifestyle and various physical and cognitive tests. The young lady conducting the survey was based at the London School of Hygiene and Tropical Medicine and she spent just over three hours with me. The tests included filming my walking speed up and down the pavement outside (not fast by this time!), lifting my arms and legs and a memory test. These were all recorded on film to assess my neurological status and I also gave blood and saliva samples.

It was explained to me beforehand that the results would be recorded but not sent back to me, although my GP was informed of my agreement to participate. The following June, I took part in some follow-up investigations which were done remotely. This mainly comprised of memory tests and lasted one hour, which I found quite tiring.

In 2016, the PFA had also been in contact with me to ask if I would like to take part in an osteoarthritis and football study, which I was again happy to do. This comprised of a series of X-rays being taken at Spire Hospital in Southampton on both my knees and ankles and was then followed up in 2020 by a further study, Foot Arthritis and Concussion in UK Soccer, again fully supported by the FA and PFA.

Although huge changes have been made since my playing days, I strongly feel the importance of taking part in these kinds of studies will help to ensure a better future for players to come, as long as the findings are implemented.

Another major concern that we must become more aware is that of a player's mental health. In an article in the *Daily Mail* on 30 June 2017, their football editor, Ian Ladyman, revealed just how close former Tottenham Hotspur defender Steven Caulker had come to committing suicide because of his problems with alcohol and gambling.

This, as we all know, was not a one-off. So many stories like this come up time and again. The question I am asking is 'Who really cares?' As I mentioned in a previous chapter, many years back, Justin Fashanu did take his own life, which, quite apart from the personal tragedy, was also a devastating blow for everyone associated with him.

Having been involved in his development from a young boy, working together on a daily basis over a considerable period of time, I personally found the news traumatic. Although he had very different problems to Steven Caulker, how much is being done today within the game to help professional footballers, past and present?

So many stories within football come up time and time again, but who really cares? Obviously, there are groups out there set up by the likes of Tony Adams at Sporting Chance. But, for all that, there are many people who are not genuine in their concern and instead only encourage the paths to destruction, which is all too easy when money is flowing and people want to be your friend. It doesn't take long for a player to become trapped in these situations.

Steven Caulker said that two of his club managers tried to help him but, to be honest, their expertise is in producing and playing successful players and teams. Any particular club may have as many as 20 to 40 professionals on their books and it is not difficult for anyone who wants to, to quite successfully hide their problems in a group of this size.

As stated previously, the manager's responsibility lies mainly with what happens on the pitch; they have more than enough to deal with there. To my mind, how refreshing it would be for every club to also have on hand at least one, or maybe two, mentors. Certainly, at the academy in Southampton we had pastoral care from Father Andrew, but how about an ex-professional with full understanding of the footballing side? He would know how a footballer's brain works and may have faced similar challenges himself, and his experiences would enable him to offer advice, assistance and help to alleviate problems unrelated to playing the game itself.

I imagine, sadly, that a lot of lower division clubs would not be happy to take on these extra costs, as they would feel the money would be better spent having an extra or better player joining the club, but to my way of thinking, that is naïve. Proper support and help in dealing with both playing and personal issues will allow players to concentrate on the job in hand; playing the game and enjoying a good, fulfilling life.

So, did football save me? Most certainly, it opened my eyes and brought me so many privileges along the way. Each chapter in this book and in my life has led me to work with so many amazing people. Many were already or have become household names. Others were, perhaps, not known to the general public. But all of them have been friends and supported me throughout various stages of my life.

However, I have certainly had my fair share of low points. I have come into contact with and, at times, fallen foul of the drinking, gambling culture that surrounds football. Also, the hangers-on purporting to be your friend. Thankfully, though, I have come out the other side and am so genuinely grateful for nearly 60 years in this amazing sport.

18.
AND ANOTHER THING ...

IF I had been more interested in my family history when I was younger, I would have found out that I could have qualified to play international football for Scotland and Sweden, as well as England. My maternal grandfather was born in Gothenburg and my maternal great grandfather was born in Scotland. We will never know if I might have been successful!

* * *

Amusing, serious, poignant, challenging and sometimes downright awkward moments occur at all football clubs, and this was certainly the case during my playing and coaching career. After all, a football club is about far more than the game itself. It is like a family, with all the ups, downs and aspects of life we all face day to day. We certainly had some very funny times at Stockport and it's probably just as well I can't remember more of them because they would probably not be suitable for publication!

* * *

Having just been made first-team coach at Manchester City, I travelled by train from Norwich to watch City play Birmingham to get an idea of their style of play and the players I would be working with. I was wearing a Bob Stokoe-style white raincoat and thinking I looked the part but surprise, surprise, I slept all the way to Manchester. City's secretary Bernard Halford probably thought he was picking up a United States gangster at Piccadilly Station, but I went straight into working mode and started to plan all the upcoming training sessions to show I was for real.

* * *

Lots of knowledge and experience are good, but training and coaching methods continually evolve. I found that, to try and keep players fit in a group, certain basic running and exercises were adequate but that individuals needed individual workouts such as stamina, sprinting, weight training and, most importantly, a specific plan to enable them to peak both mentally and physically on matchdays.

There is one aspect of preparation, though, that remains as important as ever. I watched an international match the other evening and saw one of the players overstretch his hamstring straight from the kick-off and play no further part in the game. Training sessions should always start with a warm-up and at the end of the session or game there must be a warm-down to disperse lactic acid and reduce stiffness in muscle groups.

Quite a few players still do not like warming up, as they feel they are using up some of the energy they might require in the game itself. Well, the energy that international player had left the other evening was no good to him after he had done his hamstring in the first minute!

* * *

We have now moved on to a more digital age and today's scouting methods are so very different, very computer-orientated and, although I recognise myself as a bit of a dinosaur in that respect, to my way of thinking, no amount of charts and screens can take away the gut feeling of a good scout who can observe the player on the pitch performing his or her skills and recognise their ability.

* * *

I had the pleasure to play or work with so many fine players and here is my affectionate take on a very small selection of them:

Chris Baird (Southampton): I brought him over from Northern Ireland as a youngster. He found it difficult to settle in at first but, with the protection of a family environment at The Lodge, grew to become a player of international stature who took no prisoners.

James Beattie (Southampton): We saw each other most days, as we lived opposite each other in Ocean Village for a time. He moved in the end! An intelligent, powerful player who just wanted to score goals.

Wayne Bridge (Southampton): Such an asset to have in your team. On song, he was brilliant and was always an easy-going person to work with.

Joe Corrigan (Manchester City): A great guy and a wonderful presence in the City goal. Not a person to argue with, though. You just suggested things and hoped he would agree!

Jason Dodd (Southampton): Another easy-going character, as long as he liked you! I feel he could have gone further in his career. Very trustworthy and good to have in the team.

Kevin Francis (Stockport County): With his height, Kevin was brilliant up front or in defensive situations and a lot of our play at County revolved around him whilst he was at Edgeley Park.

Ted MacDougall (AFC Bournemouth and Norwich City): If Ted was in the team, I always felt that, if we passed the ball to him, then nine times out of ten he would score. I always got on all right with Ted, both on and off the field, but he was a nightmare sometimes! He was always right, but that didn't bother me. I knew who he was and what he was, a great goalscorer and an outstanding player.

Scott McDonald (Southampton): I brought him over from Australia. A hard worker and great goalscorer. Always reliable in front of goal, he reminded me of Ted MacDougall. I'm proud to say he went on to be an Australian international.

Chris Marsden (Stockport County and Southampton): Chris would rather kick you than shake your hand! Seriously though, he was our Dave Mackay, a leader who sorted things out for the team.

Carlton Palmer (Southampton): Carlton was a box of tricks on his own, not only on the field but off it as well!

Tony Powell (AFC Bournemouth and Norwich City): Formerly a boxer, hence his nickname 'Knocker'. Converted from an attacker to a defender. He played very hard but was usually fair … in his own mind!

Kevin Reeves (AFC Bournemouth, Norwich City and Manchester City): His basic asset was scoring goals, but he embraced any position he was asked to play in. Kevin had a natural ability, plenty of pace and certainly knew where the goal was. A good all-round squad member and a gem of a lad.

David Stringer (Norwich City): You always knew you could trust Dave to do what was required on or off the pitch. A real 'Steady Eddie'.

Colin Suggett (Norwich City): Every team needs someone like Colin. He would unite defence and midfield and bring midfield into play with the forwards.

Alan Gilzean, Jimmy Greaves, Dave Mackay, Jimmy Robertson, Terry Venables and **John White**. These six players were the stronghold of the Spurs team when I was there:

- Terry Venables came from Dagenham near where I lived and sometimes gave me a lift home.
- Jimmy Greaves was just a normal guy, as were the others.
- John White was one of the best two players I have ever seen in my lifetime. They first called him 'The Ghost' because he could always anticipate the next pass and be ready to receive it. John didn't score that many goals, but the amount he created was huge. Such a tragic end to his life, struck by lightning on the golf course at far too young an age.
- But the best player I ever saw was Dave Mackay. Dave would run through brick walls, never showing fear of anyone. He appeared to be as hard as nails but would always notice players who were under pressure in his team and offer help and encouragement.

* * *

Looking back as I complete this final chapter, I feel that I have been privileged to have trained and played alongside some of the most famous names in football history, to have coached many more, to have crossed the threshold and worked at some of the most legendary clubs, travelled the world and, in my eyes perhaps the most pleasing achievement, to have played my part in helping produce some of the most talented players in recent years. Had I gone into the docks and worked alongside my dad, none of this would have come about.

I began jotting down my recollections, experiences and thoughts at the age of 21 and have been adding to these notes ever since, throughout my career as a player, coach, manager, assistant manager and academy director. Was I thinking along the lines of hoping to get them put into print one day? Maybe!

I would, however, have got nowhere with this work without the invaluable help of many, many people along the way. I thank you all, it has been an incredible journey.

Sadly, as my dementia robs me of precious memories of so many of these extraordinary times, I can at least read all of this and look back through my scrapbooks, which my dad proudly kept, together with many programmes, photos and press cuttings.

I can do so with a smile and a laugh. Six times at Wembley but never on the winning side. Quite a record that!

But I have my England Schoolboys cap.

I count myself as truly blessed.

Finally, in the words of Dave Jones, who went on to manage at Wolverhampton Wanderers, Cardiff City, Sheffield Wednesday and Hartlepool after leaving Southampton … 'John wasn't just a good No.2 for me, he was a good person all-round. He wasn't just an educator in the football world, he was an educator in life.

'I loved him to bits and haven't got a bad word to say about him. We did everything together and we worked well together.

'John was meticulous in what he did. He always tried to treat people as he would like to be treated himself but could distinguish between what was good and what was not.

'Just because John was not one of the best known doesn't mean to say he wasn't the best. He just didn't get the praise he deserved.'

APPENDIX

During his playing career, **John Sainty** made first-team appearances for four different Football League clubs:

READING 1967–1970

Football League: 63 full appearances plus eight as a substitute; 19 goals

FA Cup: three full appearances; one goal

League Cup: three full appearances; one goal

AFC BOURNEMOUTH 1970–1974

Football League: 111 full appearances plus seven as a substitute; 21 goals

FA Cup: six full appearances

League Cup: ten full appearances; three goals

MANSFIELD TOWN 1972 (Loan)

Football League: three full appearances

ALDERSHOT 1974–75

Football League: 26 full appearances plus three as a substitute

FA Cup: one full appearance

ACKNOWLEDGEMENTS

In addition to all those who have contributed their own words about John, Lindsay would like to pass on special thanks to the following people for their understanding, assistance and encouragement during the completion of this book:

Jay Astley
Phil Brennan
Edward Couzens-Lake
Michelle Hampshaw
Matt Heward-Mills
Graham Hiley
Duncan Holley
Chris Lee
Keith and Christine Moulden
Graham Nickless
Terry Owens
Lorelei Reddin
Roger Ware

Front cover photograph by Colin Davies (Phil Brennan collection)

BIBLIOGRAPHY

Brennan, Phil, *The Man from Uruguay: Danny Bergara – A Footballing Journey* (Rose-Martin Publications, 2013)

Couzens-Lake, Edward, *Norwich City: The Seventies* (Amberley, 2013)

Couzens-Lake, Edward, *Norwich City: The Eighties* (Amberley, 2015)

Donovan, Mike, *Dave Mackay: Football's Braveheart* (Pitch Publishing, 2021)

Holley, Duncan and Chalk, Gary, *In That Number: A Post-War Chronicle of Southampton FC)* (Hagiology Publishing, 2003)

Hugman, Barry, *The PFA Premier and Football League Players' Records 1946–2015* (G2 Entertainment, 2015)

Jones, David, *On the Edge* (Paper Plane Publishing Ltd, 1997)

Jones, David, *No Smoke, No Fire* (Know the Score Books, 2009)

Shannon, Kevin, *Hutch: Hard Work and Belief (The Tommy Hutchinson Story)* (Pitch Publishing, 2022)

Thomas, Dave, *A Director's Tale: John Bond, Burnley and the Diaries of Director Derek Gill* (Pitch Publishing, 2022)

Vacher, Neil and MacDougall, Ted, *MacDouGOAL!: The Ted MacDougall Story* (Pitch Publishing, 2016)

Vacher, Neil, *Goal Along with the Cherries* (AFC Bournemouth, 2021)